WINNING MARKETING DECISIONS THAT GROW A BUSINESS:

How Successful Entrepreneurs Do It

About The Author

GREG BYRNE generates marketing strategies and ideas – on occasions, they're big ideas and he turns them into economic and social value through positioning and branding.

Over the period 1985 to 1988, working with Niall Crowley and Alex Spain – respectively Chairmen of the Financial Services Industry Association (FSIA) – he contributed significantly to the creation of an "industry development" agenda and successfully positioned and branded the "FSIA" as a respected and effective "industry development" forum amongst the industry's key stakeholder audiences.

His idea for FSIA member companies to "host a table of international targets" led to the first significant marketing initiative to attract international financial services companies to the Dublin International Financial Services Centre. Reportage of that event, attended by some 1,000 financial services executives, recorded it thus:

> FSIA woos the world ... Three years ago, little if anything was known about the financial services industry in this country, but with the establishment of the FSIA, Ireland is set to play an increasing and prominent role in European and international financial markets ...
>
> (Report on the FSIA London Seminar to promote the IFSC, *Stubbs Gazette*, April 1988)

Over the following the eight years (1988–1996), Greg got involved with another "big idea" – the IIB Bank/Irish Life joint venture to create a "centralised mortgage lender" for the Irish mortgage market. There, he created the "*Homeloans Business Builder*" strategy and tool-kit that educated, supported and brought about, for the first time in Ireland, nationwide distribution of mortgages through Broker & Life Office Sales Force Intermediaries. Amongst his product innovations were the "Stabilizer Homeloan" and "Flexi-Homeloan":

> The stabilizer homeloan is a clever solution to the inherent marketing problem of the fixed rate mortgage, the failure of the fixed rate to give customers the benefit of any declines in the underlying level of interest rates ... (*The Irish Times*, 27 September 1990)

> Irish life homeloans' flexible new mortgage package is a step in the right direction. The flexibility is welcome and should be copied by other institutions ... Home-buyers should expect more of this kind of flexibility from their lenders ... (*Evening Herald*, 9 November 1994)

During his four years with Irish Life, the country's largest life assurance company,

Greg researched and developed a new brand position for the retail business, centred on a differentiated customer value proposition and supported by new customer CRM and product development processes for consistent delivery of the new brand position. The repositioning of the entire life assurance suite of products in "plain English", duly crystal marked and with an "honesty mark", was an industry first.

> Irish Life has laid down a new standard for customer information that others should be wasting no time in adopting ... The result is a customer brochure like no other on the Irish Market ... (*The Irish Times*, 5 June 1998)

From 2000 to 2004, Greg created a leadership brand position for Ernst & Young Ireland in the vibrant entrepreneurial market, centred on an innovative and distinctive value proposition of business development support and brand build for Ireland's high-potential entrepreneurs in the Ernst & Young Entrepreneur Of The Year ® Awards Programme. After just two years, the brand attracted more than 120 nominees annually entering the programme. Approaching 700 business leaders, influencers and guests attend the Awards Banquet and more than 500,000 people watched the TV programmes in 2003.

> Ernst & Young raised the bar for corporate sponsorship when they managed to get their annual Entrepreneur Of The Year awards presentation onto RTE ... only pedigree acts need apply ... E&Y's annual awards are now firmly established ... (*Business Plus Magazine*, 2001)

> E&Y are to be congratulated on their initiative in identifying and supporting this sector ..." (Former Managing Partner – KPMG)

> ... a superbly professional event ... your commitment and acknowledgement of the Sector acts as a key cornerstone in fostering continued drive and determination in many an up and coming entrepreneur ... (Awards Banquet Guest, 2003)

> I really must say that I have not attended a function like it in some time. It was absolutely fascinating to see how all the various nominees had brought their fledgling plans to fruition. Ernst & Young can be very proud of themselves for the part they play in encouraging entrepreneurs to follow their hopes and dreams...Ernst & Young can also be proud of the show they put on ... (Awards Banquet Guest, 2003)

Greg now provides strategic marketing planning consultancy to the high-potential entrepreneur community in Ireland and is currently creating a dedicated online resource – www.marketing4entrepreneurs.com – providing insights, guides and tools for entrepreneurs.

This is his first book.

Winning Marketing Decisions that Grow a Business: How Successful Entrepreneurs Do It

"... a real tour de force **in defining and refining that route to market."**

"Modern entrepreneurs are far too consumed with their businesses and business ideas to consult a textbook, but they do need advice and guidance to assist them in dilemmas where their experience is patchy. The concept of a roadmap rather than a textbook is ideal for busy and impatient business people who need a reference point, and this book provides the perfect answer to those needing inspiration to resolve a critical marketing issue.

"Greg Byrne's experience in assisting Irish entrepreneurs to achieve scale is very rich and should provide lessons for aspiring start-ups worldwide. A major issue in the dotcom collapse has been an inability of technology entrepreneurs to plan and execute a route to market for their products. This roadmap is a real tour de force in defining and refining that route to market."

PAT MAHER, Executive Director, Enterprise Ireland
Enterprise Ireland is the national organisation with responsibility for accelerating Ireland's national and regional development and focuses its resources on companies that are characterised by high levels of ambition, innovation and commitment to international growth.

"... essential and timely reading for any entrepreneur or senior manager in a business start-up."

"Great marketing is a core element of great start-ups and Winning Marketing Decisions that Grow a Business provides an excellent roadmap for great marketing. The book is essential and timely reading for any entrepreneur or senior manager in a business start-up.

"While many have written about the role of marketing in organisations there have been surprisingly few contributions to the particular issues and challenges of marketing in the frenetic environment of a start-up business. Starts-ups are subject to unique and complex challenges; frequently the standard marketing models suited to large corporations are inapplicable. However, as is clearly demonstrated here, marketing can and must play a central role in early-stage growth and development.

"This book details both the why and the how of successful entrepreneurial marketing. Readers are given insights into the changing requirements of successful marketing across the three phases of company growth. It is a valuable resource that will assist entrepreneurs in predicting and pre-empting the marketing challenges that confront their companies as they move through the three growth phases."

DON O'SULLIVAN, Lecturer in Marketing, University College Cork

Don joined UCC in 1992 and lectures in the ICT sector and the measurement of marketing performance. He has been a visiting lecturer at the University of Notre Dame in the USA and the University of Dushanbe in Tajikistan (CIS). He is a member of the editorial review board for Advances in Business Marketing and Purchasing. He is an award-winning case writer. His professional memberships include the European Marketing Academy and the Irish Marketing Teachers Association. He has just spent four years in industry where he was head of strategic marketing at TechBrad, a marketing services company focused on the European technology sector. He is enrolled for a Doctorate at UCC researching the measurement of marketing performance.

"... a welcome addition to the tool-kit of entrepreneurs focused on growing their business in competitive global markets."

"Here at last is a simple and well-sequenced resource to help young entrepreneurs. Its templates and checklists are easy to follow and adapt as the business grows. It will be of particular help to the entrepreneur coming from a technical or product background.

This book is really a field-book (containing notes from the field) of "stuff that works", compiled by an experienced sales and marketing practitioner. It includes valuable input from successful Irish and International companies. It reflects new maturity and wisdom and is a welcome addition to the tool-kit of entrepreneurs focused on growing their business in competitive global markets."

JOE O'KEEFFE, BE, MEd, Chartered FCIPD

Joe is a graduate of the National University of Ireland, with a BE in Electrical Engineering (1964) and also a graduate of the General Electric (USA) Management Program. Joe worked as HR, Engineering & Operations Manager in GE's Semiconductor Products Department. His experience includes General Manager and MD with some of the world's best-managed companies, including Emerson Electric, AT&T and Apple Computer (in Ireland and USA). Joe currently serves on a number of corporate boards. He also works as a mentor with Enterprise Ireland and companies in the IT sector. He has participated in an International Development Ireland (IDI) team involved in the restructuring of the Hungarian telecommunications industry.

"... fills a clear market gap and is a must-have part of the tool-kit for early stage entrepreneurs and their advisors."

"Greg Byrne's marketing field-book is timely and impressive. It is timely because it addresses the fundamental reason why so many start-up companies fail to reach their full potential. He hits the nail on the head by highlighting the requirement for start-ups to make the transition from the very practical early stage product-led approach to the more complex market-led approach, which is critical to future growth and success.

Experience shows that most start-ups either collapse or reach a ceiling beyond which they can't proceed because they have not internalised and implemented a strategic marketing approach.

"The book is impressive because the author practises what he preaches. It is a good example of do as I say and do as I do. He de-mystifies a complex process and provides an excellent guide and workbook using charts, templates and checklists which will enable all practitioners to draw value from the content.

"Greg Byrne's book fills a clear market gap and is a must-have part of the tool-kit for early stage entrepreneurs and their advisors."

KEVIN THOMPSTONE, Chief Executive, Shannon Development
Shannon Development is Ireland's only dedicated regional development company, with a brief to generate industry, tourism and rural development in the wider Shannon area, known as the Shannon Region. Shannon Development is focused on developing and strengthening companies' capability and competitiveness in the global economy.

"The company sells stuff they cannot build or they build stuff they cannot sell."

"It looks like you have covered the ground pretty thoroughly. It seems that in most of the businesses – big or small, new or old – that I study, it is pretty simple things that cause the biggest problems: the company sells stuff they can not build or they build stuff that they can not sell. And rather than hire someone who knows what to do by reflex, they try to learn-on-the-job, all too often running out of either money or hope in the process. It looks like you talk about all of these issues. Good luck with your book and with the Irish entrepreneurial community."

PROFESSOR JOSEPH B. LASSITER III, Harvard Business School
Author of *Entrepreneurial Marketing: Learning from High-Potential Ventures*, Harvard Business School 9-803-036 Paper, October 2003.

"... great insights from the sharp end into the role of marketing in growing businesses"

"There is a mystique about entrepreneurs and how their minds work. This book uses real-life examples from Ireland and abroad from those who have made their mark, and helps us to understand the processes of entrepreneurial thought. We are offered some great insights from the sharp end into the role of marketing in growing businesses."

LIAM NELLIS, Chief Executive, InterTradeIreland
InterTradeIreland's mission is to lead the development of the island economy through distinctive knowledge-based interventions which will produce significant returns in the areas of cross-border trade and business development.

Winning Marketing Decisions that Grow a Business:

How Successful Entrepreneurs Do It

GREG BYRNE

The Three Little Pigs Co.
TURN-KEY MARKETING FOR ENTREPRENEURS

BLACKHALL
Publishing

This book was typeset by Ashfield Typesetting Services for

BLACKHALL PUBLISHING
27 Carysfort Avenue
Blackrock
Co. Dublin
Ireland

e-mail: info@blackhallpublishing.com
www.blackhallpublishing.com

ISBN: 1 842180 71 1 (HB)
1 842180 73 8 (PB)

A catalogue record for this book is available from the British Library.

Printed in Ireland by
ColourBooks Ltd

DEDICATION

To my wife Margaret and daughters Hilary, Aoife and Hannah-B:
I couldn't be more blessed

To my parents Patricia and Michael, and sisters Molly and Caroline:
Always my supporters

For my sister Hilary and brother Martin:
Remembered

The author's royalty proceeds go to Our Lady's
Hospital for Sick Children

Contents

LIST OF FIGURES

LIST OF TEMPLATES

Chapter 2
Template 1: PEST Analysis for Market Drivers and Market Strategy
Template 2: Market Segmentation

Chapter 3
Template 3: Market Research Process
Template 4: Channel Decision Process
Template 5: Advertising Campaign Planning Process
Template 6: Request for Proposal for Media Relations Services to
          Company X
Template 7: Direct Mail Marketing
Template 8: Brand/Product Position Statement – To Drive All Marketing
          Communications – During the Emerging Stage
Template 9: Corporate Brand: Integrated Marketing Communication
          Programme for Start Up and Emerging Stage

Chapter 4
Template 8: Corporate Brand/Product Position Statement – To Drive All
          Marketing Communications – During the Rapid Growth Stage
Template 9: Corporate Brand – Integrated Marketing Communication
          Programme for Rapid Growth and Next Level Stages
Template 10: Corporate Brand Position Development Process
Template 11: Advertising Agency Creative Brief and Media Planning
Template 12: Corporate Brand Position Experience Programme
Template 13: Product Positioning Development and Launch Process
Template 14: Key Account Management
Template 15: Intermediary Corporate Brand Positioning Development
          Process
Template 16: International Expansion Strategy Development
Template 17: Product Adaptation for International Markets

Chapter 5
Template 18: DPM Analysis of Market Positions and Market Attractiveness
Template 19: Market Plan Document
Template 20: Marketing Planning Process: Insights, Tips and Templates

List of Examples

List of Checklists

List of Tables

Foreword

from Denis O'Brien

Dear Reader,

It is remarkable that it has taken until now to bring entrepreneurs and "marketing" together for an insight into what makes new ventures grow.

Remarkable in the sense that when you stand back and think about the characteristics of a good entrepreneur and a good marketer and what both can do for a new venture – you can describe them in almost the exact same way.

Great entrepreneurs and great marketers are both foremost opportunity oriented in mindset and they share an empathy to see things from the customer's point of view. They have an imagination and creativity to bring about sustainable advantage and clear market positioning. They have a deep passion about what they do, ranging to competitive aggression, and it drives both characters to "win". Both know that it takes time for things to take effect, so patience and perseverance are essential. Both know that the "giving" of value and help to others for free creates the "getting" that invariably follows and sustains the venture. Put the two together, build them into a new entrepreneurial venture and you substantially increase the odds for success.

The Winning Marketing Decisions that Grow a Business – How Successful Entrepreneurs Do It

This book for the first time brings "marketing" and entrepreneurs together. It charts, in a concise, practical and understandable way, the road map of what lies ahead for the early stage entrepreneur and the key marketing decisions that must be made. Of particular value to the time-constrained, multi-tasking entrepreneur is its sequenced approach to providing the marketing decision-making guidance for successfully reaching a served international market leadership position.

In the frenetic start up/emerging stage of the venture, it is all about survival and the need to aggressively deploy all available, tactical "push" marketing and sales techniques – like PR, personal selling and promotions. However, in the rapid growth stage, the entrepreneur must shift the business from "product push" to a "market-led" business based on a differentiated brand positioning. In this stage of growth, there is a whole new set of decisions that must now be taken if the venture is to progress further to the served market leadership level.

With insights from successful entrepreneurs from around the globe revealing their best marketing strategies, tactics and actions with field-proven charts/templates providing the guidance and a framework for developing marketing strategies and making winning marketing decisions at each growth stage and with checklists to ensure effective and efficient implementation – this resource is required reading for all early stage entrepreneurs

DENIS O'BRIEN
Chairman, Digicel Limited
Ernst & Young Entrepreneur Of The Year® Ireland 1998

Foreword

from Gregory K. Ericksen

Dear Reader,

Since 1986, when the Ernst & Young Entrepreneur Of The Year program was launched, we have had the privilege of honouring thousands of entrepreneurs worldwide for their successes in creating and growing new ventures. These entrepreneurs represent a multitude of countries and numerous industries. Despite the diversity among these entrepreneurs, however, one common theme emerges: all have had sound marketing strategies throughout the life cycles of their ventures.

Indeed, one thing our Entrepreneur Of The Year award winners have taught us is that effective marketing is at the very core of entrepreneurial success. From the initial stages of identifying an opportunity to raising capital, hiring the team, developing the main products or services, cultivating key relationships with suppliers, building a strong customer base and so on as the company evolves, successful entrepreneurs stay focused on their company's primary goal – to meet customer needs at a profit. While this may seem like a simple and obvious goal, the road to entrepreneurial success is littered with companies that have failed because they somehow either forgot about their customers or lost touch with them along the way. This can happen for many reasons: for example, overly enthusiastic developers enamoured of features or investors focused exclusively on short-term pay-offs. In fact, as the author of this book points out, it is estimated that some 60 per cent of new companies fail because of poor marketing.

Successful entrepreneurs, on the other hand, have a deep understanding of the market. They understand what their customers really want, need, fear, value and so on, and they do not let anything distract them. Successful entrepreneurs also understand marketing's big picture. They understand the size of their market, the competition, the barriers to entry and, overall, the feasibility of actually delivering a new product or service at a price the market will bear. Successful entrepreneurs are also able to overcome market resistance, often the case with something new and unproven. The ability to overcome market resistance is particularly critical where the risks of product failure are great, as in the medical field.

Moreover, successful entrepreneurs are able to change direction rapidly in response to market feedback, even when this entails a total overhaul of the organisation from hiring to operations and beyond. Overall, as the author of this book notes, successful entrepreneurs do not think of marketing as mere "sales support". They understand that good marketing is a complex and dynamic process that must continually evolve in response to customers, competitors and others in the market.

To manage all of this well, the entrepreneur must create a strong feedback loop linking marketing with other core functions. As a result, while marketing is critical for any firm, young or old, it can mean the difference between success and failure, life and death for a start-up. And the challenges entrepreneurs face can be overwhelming, far greater than what established firms face. For example, unlike established firms, entrepreneurs cannot rely on a brand. They cannot use profits from existing products or services to market new ones. They cannot rely on an existing customer base. They cannot rely on existing distribution channels, and so on. And if barriers to entry are low and established firms enter their market, entrepreneurs have to compete with firms that do have a brand, that can channel profits from other lines into marketing, that do have a customer base, etc. Like Ginger Rogers, entrepreneurs have to do everything the established firms do when it comes to marketing only they have to do it "backwards and in high heels".

Clearly, then, marketing is a critical issue for entrepreneurs. While much ink has been spilled on the marketing issues facing large established firms, surprisingly little has been written to address the particular marketing challenges entrepreneurs face. This book helps fill that gap. Written by a long time Ernst & Young colleague with years of experience advising entrepreneurs from diverse industries, the book offers a no-nonsense guide to entrepreneurial marketing. Through what the author describes as the three stages of entrepreneurial development – start-up, emerging and rapid growth – the book provides time-tested strategies for dealing with marketing issues likely to confront an entrepreneur at every step along the way. And it is written not as an academic textbook on marketing but rather as a kind of quick, one-stop reference for the multi-tasking, beyond-busy entrepreneur. Finally, the book offers an international perspective, which should prove increasingly useful as markets become more connected and firms ever more global in scope.

In short, marketing matters. And the entrepreneur who understands this today will have a greatly improved chance of becoming the successful entrepreneur of tomorrow. This book can serve as a kind of field guide for staying out of the woods and on the path to entrepreneurial success.

GREGORY K. ERICKSEN
Ernst & Young Global Director
Entrepreneur Of The Year

Acknowledgements

Sincerest thanks to:

Many friends, colleagues, visionaries and mentors, in effect, created this effort to help early stage entrepreneurs make it to the next level. Some inspired it. Four made me do it. Others got involved in blind faith – but with the same passion to help entrepreneurs as I have. And still more have been involved because I have learned so much from them in my career to date.

Those who inspired – my parents, Michael and Patricia Byrne, the two Chairmen of the FSIA, Niall Crowley (RIP) and Alex Spain and also Jean Wood, former CEO of Irish Life Assurance and John Farrell. They epitomised for me the "big idea" and building for a greater common good.

The four who "made me" do it with their sustaining encouragement, were Cormac Hanley of Oasis Design – probably one of the most creative designers I have ever met – Joe O'Keefe, Pat Maher and Fionan Murray, a great friend.

Those who joined in the blind faith that I could do justice in this book to their passion to help entrepreneurs make it are: Denis O'Brien, Chairman of Digicel and Entrepreneur Of The Year 1998, Ireland, Greg Ericksen, Ernst & Young Global Leader of Entrepreneur Of The Year, Mark Bezner, OLYMP Bezner GmbH, Peter Conlon, Xsil Ltd, Monica Eisinger, MIND CTI Ltd, Angela Kennedy Megazyme International, Gerry McCaughey, Century Homes & Industry Entrepreneur Of The Year 2003, Ireland, Martin McVicar, Combilift Ltd & Entrepreneur Of The Year 2001, Ireland, Terence Monaghan, BetaTHERM Sensors, Padraig O'Ceidigh, Aer Arann & Entrepreneur Of The Year 2002, Ireland, Lirio Albino Parisotto, Videolar & Entrepreneur Of The Year 2002, Brazil, Mario Moretti Polegato, Geox International Srl & Entrepreneur Of The Year 2002, Italy, Richard Reed, Innocent Drinks & Young Entrepreneur Of The Year 2003, United Kingdom and Les Schirato of Cantarella Bros. Pty Ltd & Retail, Consumer & Industrial Products Entrepreneur Of The Year 2001, Australia.

Colleagues in Ernst & Young who made it possible were: Richard Burton, David Wilkinson, Markus Seiz, Mitizy Kauperman, Gigi Chow, Yifat Adoram and Cristina Martin and to Enda Kelly who made it hugely enjoyable to work with and learn from entrepreneurs, together.

Finally, Brian Mac Manus in IIB Finance Group and Sara Denby Jones & Rosi McMurray of the pFour Consultancy – for all of the marketing experience they imparted and facilitated.

Beannacht Dé

Preface

Successful entrepreneurs grow their businesses through three distinct evolutionary stages – start up, emerging and rapid growth – to reach and re-invent their served (international) market leadership. In so doing, they make a multitude of "winning decisions" at different stages and across a wide spectrum of business drivers.

Others are not as successful in their venture – and the principal cause is marketing. It is reckoned that some 60 per cent of new ventures fail because of bad marketing decisions ... in some ventures the marketing decisions are never made ... in others they are made too late ... and many entrepreneurs struggle to build internally or buy-in the right marketing capability to evolve from a product-led start up into the market-led business that is needed for leadership position.

Generating the original big idea takes an entrepreneur's vision, creativity and persistence. Turning that into a leadership brand takes innovative, creative and disciplined marketing.

This book provides guidance to making the winning marketing decisions that grow a business. The key decisions are addressed in a sequence that maps onto the business growth path ahead. The aim is to alert and support the entrepreneur on each set of marketing strategies and actions to take, relevant to each of the three stages of development.

Figure 1: *The Four Go-To-Market Processes*

1. Systematically gathering **market intelligence** and profitably **segmenting** marketplaces

2. Powerfully **positioning** and creating differentiated **brands** for the business and its products for sustainable competitive advantage

3. Developing and managing all **channels** to market

4. Reaching target audiences cost-effectively with **integrated marketing communications** and winning **selling** actions

The winning marketing decisions that grow a business are made across all four go-to-market drivers of business growth and value. In the book, there are:

- **Templates** to provide guidance and a framework for developing the right marketing strategies and making winning marketing decisions in each driver area.

- **Insights** from successful entrepreneurs from around the globe that reveal the strategies, tactics and actions they took and are taking to grow their businesses.

- **Checklists** that can be used for ensuring effective and efficient implementation of the key marketing strategies in each driver area and at each of the three growth stages.

By tackling the marketing task in stages, by using the practical templates and checklists and by learning from the insights of other successful entrepreneurs; this field-book will hopefully compress the learning curve and enhance the mastery of marketing in entrepreneurial ventures. If this is achieved, then the odds for success are much better. And everyone wins.

THE MISSING MARKETING

Failure to Transition from Product Focus to a Brand Positioning

Early and emerging stage entrepreneurs often fail to transition the business from a product/sales-led approach (necessary to get it off the ground) to the market-led approach needed to grow the business to the next level of success. Products are (relatively) easily copied and competed against and are not a solid basis for sustainable competitive advantage. In adopting a market-led approach, successful companies generate sustainable advantage by developing a differentiated and compelling brand positioning and increasingly they enhance this by innovation in areas other than product, for example, in new market channel strategies

Lack of Understanding of Marketing

A frequently held view is that marketing is "simple" – it is about advertising, it is about brochures and it is about sales support. If that is the understood role of marketing, then it is not surprising that business stalling and/or terminating changes are missed by the company (because there is no systematic market focus and gathering of market intelligence), new customer needs are left unmet and competitor actions are not responded to. This is a recipe for failure.

Finance First, Marketing Later

Because Finance is "complex", entrepreneurs will, at an early stage, invest time and effort to understand and manage it as a critical business function. Often, "complex" is more understood than "simple", because more time is committed to understanding the complex matter. Marketing, on the other hand, is not usually mapped or looked at in process or strategic terms. This reinforces the "marketing is simple" perception and therefore its often lengthy absence from the top team. As a result, very often "funding rounds" and amounts sought by entrepreneurs are divorced from an understanding of the real scale of marketing investment required to build brand.

First Product a Winner, but then ...

It is often the case that an entrepreneur comes out of an industry and company that they have worked in and they are initially armed with a deep understanding of the market's problems around a particular product area. Their frustrations and visions drive them to create their own solutions and businesses. They set up and build their solution for the known problem, they focus on sales, they create awareness/leads through industry trade/exhibitions shows and their first product is a success. The next product, however, is less so and then the next product dies. Why?

The entrepreneur has become a vendor and the business is product/sales led. He/she is no longer in the market. The intimate and detailed market knowledge that they had is eroding. Sales staff, recruited along the way, are product-focussed and rewarded. They do not have the market knowledge. If there are marketing staff, they are "sales support" focussed. They are sucked into tactical campaigns around product and they are not strategic in or perhaps capable of acquiring the key market knowledge and intelligence about customer needs, competitor actions and marketing environment changes.

Promoting Internal Marketing Staff ...

Many companies, as they go through the rapid growth stage in their evolution, will cope by promoting internally, because of ease/convenience and because they cannot afford to hire a professional externally. The potential issue with internal candidates filling the marketing slot is the challenge in finding marketing professionals who have the requisite experience and skill-set in devising and branding new corporate and new product positioning to compete in often times discontinuous markets, where significant change is required of the buyer. Marketing staff in early stage entrepreneurial businesses often do not have this experience and tacit know-how.

THE HARD QUESTION

Ask for the written *Customer Value Proposition* (or *Product Positioning*) and its market-originated, clear statement of:

- **Who** is the target customer?
- **What** is the product category? (What does it do or replace?)
- **What** is the unique benefit versus competitors? (Customer's key benefit having regard to their key needs/values)
- **Why** should the target customer believe you? (What is the proof?)

and the **marketing processes** that underpin its ongoing evolution!

If they are not there, there is "missing marketing" and the venture is at risk. Revenue growth will likely decelerate and plateau. Achieving new levels of growth, through market opportunities and internationalisation, will be undermined.

NEXT CHAPTER

In the next chapter, each of the three stages of growth – start-up/emerging, rapid growth and next level – are examined in terms of the typical company characteristics that prevail, the major business goals targeted and the four key marketing decision areas are mapped onto the journey *vis* market intelligence, brand positioning, channels and communication.

Chapter 1

What Lies Ahead: The Roadmap and Stages of Growth

INTRODUCTION

In today's compressed timelines and markets, entrepreneurial growth companies need to envision themselves, from the start, as the large, successful business they are to become. From an early stage they need to work on the "how" to get there. This chapter sets out what lies ahead for the early stage entrepreneur as they evolve their business through the three stages of growth – start up/emerging, rapid growth and next level – that typically span an initial three- to seven-year period of growth. Marketing is of critical importance to the success of entrepreneurial ventures.

Successful entrepreneurs make a series of winning marketing decisions in four areas – marketing intelligence, brand positioning, channels and communications – and they apply these decisions across the five drivers of growth and value as the venture evolves through its three stages – start up/emerging, rapid growth and next level.

Figure 1.1: *Importance of Marketing for Business Success*

Importance of Marketing

"... Compared to other business functions, marketing has been rated as much more important to the new venture's prosperity. Fourteen venture capitalists who backed more than 200 ventures rated the importance of business functions to the success of the enterprise. The marketing function was rated 6.7 on a scale of 7.0, higher than any other business function. In-depth interviews with the same venture capitalists concluded that venture failure rates can be reduced as much as 60 per cent using pre-venture marketing analysis ..."

Entrepreneurial Marketing: Lessons from Wharton's Pioneering MBA Course. February 2001. Leonard M. Lodish, Howard Lee Morgan and Amy Kallianpur.

Marketing is key to business strategy, it has a critical impact on (brand and revenue generating) operational processes and it is a key business management function. It will also play an important role in presenting the venture to potential investors and financiers, who will look for evidence of strong market-led growth foundations. For example, Tech Coast Angels (an American Venture Capital Group) look for an eleven-slide presentation from entrepreneurs seeking funding – virtually all slides are marketing dependent.

Figure 1.2: *Marketing Is Key when Presenting to Funders*

Eleven *must-have* slides

1. **Cover** – Business positioning statement
2. **Market** – The need and what customers have it
3. **Solution** – Product, core benefit, protectable technology(ies)
4. **Competitive Position** – Who they are and your defences
5. **Marketing/Sales/Support** – Channels and skills needed
6. **Business Strategy** – How you plan to grow beyond launch
7. **Financial Projections** – The usual spreadsheets
8. **Funding Sought** – Amount, comparables, use of funds
9. **Management** – Relevant experience
10. **Milestones** – Product launch, next funding, breakeven, for example
11. **Exit Strategy** – IPO/acquisition (who?)

THE ENTREPRENEUR'S ROADMAP: GROWTH STAGES AND WINNING MARKETING DECISIONS

This is not a marketing A-Z inviting a very busy, multi-tasking entrepreneur to take in all things "marketing". Rather, it takes the entrepreneurs' roadmap of growth over three stages of evolution and plots for each stage in sequence – the critical marketing strategies, processes and actions as used by successful entrepreneurs and by the author in his business services/financial services new ventures. This means that a start up/emerging stage entrepreneur can look ahead and internalise these in the business of decision making as and when needed to drive the development of the business from a product-solution-oriented start up through to served-market leader/next level.

Figure 1.3: *Winning Marketing Decisions and Growth Stage Map*

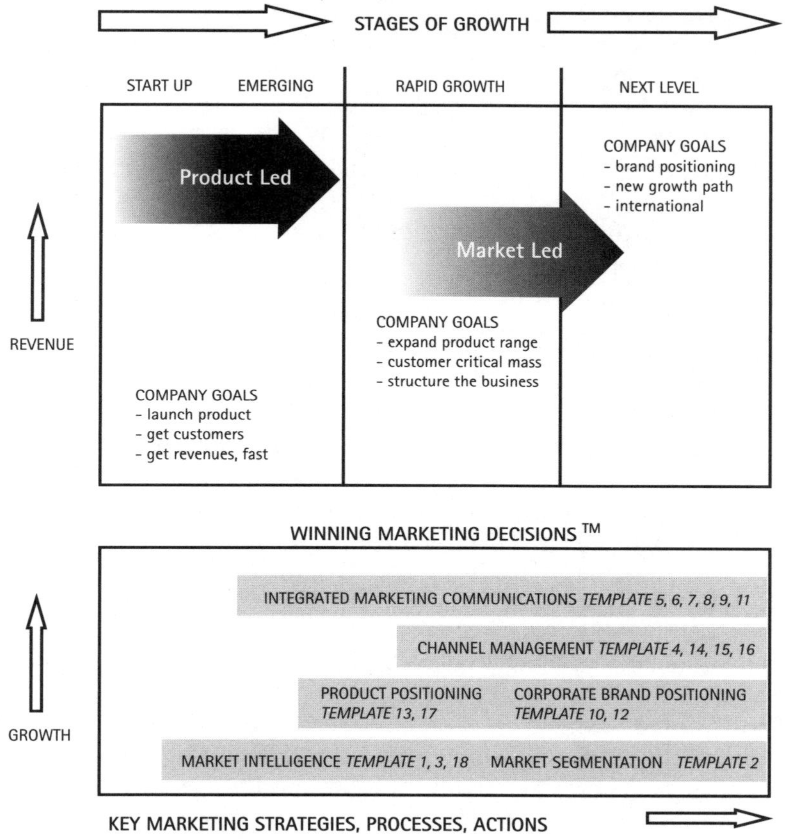

STAGES OF GROWTH

| START UP | EMERGING | RAPID GROWTH | NEXT LEVEL |

REVENUE

Product Led

Market Led

COMPANY GOALS
- brand positioning
- new growth path
- international

COMPANY GOALS
- expand product range
- customer critical mass
- structure the business

COMPANY GOALS
- launch product
- get customers
- get revenues, fast

WINNING MARKETING DECISIONS ™

GROWTH

INTEGRATED MARKETING COMMUNICATIONS *TEMPLATE 5, 6, 7, 8, 9, 11*

CHANNEL MANAGEMENT *TEMPLATE 4, 14, 15, 16*

PRODUCT POSITIONING *TEMPLATE 13, 17*　　CORPORATE BRAND POSITIONING *TEMPLATE 10, 12*

MARKET INTELLIGENCE *TEMPLATE 1, 3, 18*　　MARKET SEGMENTATION *TEMPLATE 2*

KEY MARKETING STRATEGIES, PROCESSES, ACTIONS

STAGES OF ENTERPRISE EVOLUTION

Start Up and Emerging Stage

Company Goals

- Launch new product that is different
- Capture initial customer accounts and commercialise
- Get revenues flowing in to fund sales push

Company Characteristics

The earliest phase of the entrepreneurial enterprise, typically the first three to five years after establishment, is driven by the imperative of making sales. Without sales, there is no survival. Activities are constrained by limited financial resources. The market is approached in a random and disorganised way initially. Low-hanging fruit is the objective. Ingenuity substitutes for capital resources. Flexibility with an absence of policy on "how things are done" generates creativity. Often, the formal business plan (for seed/first-round funding) is irrelevant to the reality. New opportunities emerge and original market and product concepts can change significantly. The entrepreneur leads the sales charge to market.

Key Marketing Strategies and Decisions

- Market intelligence (Template 1, 3)
- Market segmentation (Template 2)
- Corporate brand positioning
- Product positioning
- Channel management (Template 4)
- Integrated marketing communications programme (Template 5, 6, 7, 8, 9)

Rapid Growth Stage

Company Goals

- Extend/amend product range, with the second and third new extensions
- Create brand position
- Gain critical mass of customers and secure recurring revenues
- Organise and structure the business around the brand

Company Characteristics

Sales and customers reach a critical mass. Employee numbers are now becoming significant – upwards of 70 to 100 staff. The company has found a niche and a formula for repeat business. Successful business patterns replace *ad hoc* experimentation and not knowing where the next piece of business will come from. Whereas sales was crucial during the start up and emerging stage, the imperative now shifts towards developing the company's brand position in the market and an operational infrastructure with the capability to sustain growth as the "hot product" fades and the initial team moves on. As the number of clients, employees and transactions increases, along with organisational complexity, the business must focus on operations and, in particular, must understand which processes are critical to the brand and revenue growth. Functional departments emerge, such as finance, marketing, sales, IT, HR and operations/production. Business planning now becomes critical.

Key Marketing Strategies and Decisions

- Market intelligence (Template 3)
- Market segmentation and targeting
- Corporate brand positioning development (Template 10)
- New product positioning development process (Template 13, 17)
- Channel management (Template/process 14, 15)
- Internationalisation (Template/process 16, 17)
- Integrated marketing communications programme (Template 8, 9)

Next Level Stage

Company Goals

- Move to a new level of growth and success
- Leadership brand position in market(s)
- Internationalisation

Company Characteristics

At this point, one of three things happens: the business plateaus, reaching its internal limitation to growth, the business declines and fails or the company experiences a breakthrough by redefining its business strategies, structures and processes. It marks a crossroads, sometimes seeing the founder/entrepreneur moving on. If this stage is managed well, the company begins a new cycle on the growth curve: serving new opportunities for profitability, with less intense competition.

External factors often play a significant role in hurling an unsuspecting company into the next level stage. New competitors, new technologies, new industry formations and changing customer demands can all bring about the growth break point. Internal factors can also contribute, for example a lack of management depth with the required professional management experience to take the business forward.

Key Marketing Strategies and Decisions

- Directional Policy Matrix (DPM) analysis (Template 18)
- Marketing planning (Template 19, 20)

MARKETING DECISIONS/GROWTH DRIVERS MATRIX

The four sets of marketing decisions are applied by successful entrepreneurial growth companies to the five key growth drivers that

5

accelerate growth, create significant value and enable them to excel in the marketplace. In brief, these growth drivers are:

Market-Led Growth Strategies

From start up to exit and value realisation, brand is the entrepreneur's most important business growth strategy. It facilitates successful market entry at the start up stage, it provides the mechanism and lever for structuring the business in the rapid growth stage and it becomes the value to be realised by the entrepreneur at the next level stage. In addition, throughout the venture's development growth path, it is a beacon for its corporate governance.

Operating Infrastructure

Key business processes to deliver the brand position and secure revenue growth are continually mapped and re-engineered, and enabling systems are put in place to implement the brand and revenue model.

Capital and Funding

Capitalisation planning is done three to five years ahead and the focus includes creating intellectual capital, such as the corporate brand, key customer list, patents and technology. A powerful brand position is a key appraisal criterion for the investment community.

Managing the Business

Strategic business planning incorporates strategic marketing planning to establish/support the brand platform for managing growth.

Wealth Building and Retention

Planning from the outset for exit and/or succession.

SUMMARY

Marketing is a critical strategic and operational function for the entrepreneurial venture. It touches every driver of value for a venture and to be successful, entrepreneurs must make winning marketing decisions across the four key areas at each of the three stages. In Chapter 2, we will look at the foundation to winning marketing decision making – gathering marketing intelligence to understand customer needs, identify key competitor weaknesses and how the entrepreneur's venture strengths can then be used to realise a strategic competitive advantage.

Figure 1.4: *Business Growth Driver Matrix*

Growth Drivers	GROWTH STAGES			
	Start Up	Emerging	Rapid Growth	Next Level
Market-led growth strategies	Product	Sales	Brand	New markets
Operating infrastructure	"Plan"	*Ad hoc*	Brand delivery	Strategic marketing planning
Capital and funding	Launch	Commercial	Position	Extend
Managing the business	Entrepreneur	Initial team	Replacement team	Multi-location
Wealth building and retention	Value in product	Value in products	Value in market position	Exit IPO trade sale

WINNING DECISIONS			
Marketing intelligence	Brand positioning	Channels to markets	Communications & selling

7

Chapter 2

The Journey's Engine: Market Intelligence and Segmentation

INTRODUCTION

Market intelligence on customers, competitors and the marketing environment is the foundation to making the right decisions on brand positioning, channels and communications for each of the three stages of growth. In this chapter, we review the use of primary and secondary research and explain the market segmentation process, which is key to effective customer targeting.

Firms that pay close attention to customers, competitors and their marketing environment by systematically gathering and analysing key information are better placed to make the right strategic development decisions and grow. Successful companies use the marketplace as their source of growth strategies.

Markets are different to other environments that companies operate in: they are invariably dynamic and their drivers of change are diverse. In such an unstable market environment, it is easy to lose touch with customers and conditions in markets. Moreover, to survive and thrive companies have to develop new strategies, launch new products, target new markets and defend existing market positions. Therefore, the need for detailed, up-to-date knowledge is a critical success factor.

The link between market intelligence and business growth in entrepreneurial companies has been confirmed, by Business Horizons (1994) for example. "Stalled growth companies" fail to grow beyond the start up/emerging stage; the management traits in Figure 2.1 are the key characteristics to "growing companies".

Similarly, in research done by Edward B. Roberts (1991), it was established that successful companies transitioned from a technological/product orientation to a marketing and strategic orientation. The externally focused companies invested in a marketing department and market research and they integrated marketing planning into strategic planning.

Figure 2.1: *Stalled Versus Growing Companies*

Stalled Growth	Growing Companies
Sales/product-driven approach	Marketing-driven approach
Internally focussed	Externally focussed
Modest investment in market research	Systematic market research
No strategic marketing management	Marketing function/department
Small change/evolution in original market concept, positioning	Evolving positioning

Source: *Business Horizons*, Jan/Feb 1994, cited in James B. Wood, with Larry Rothstein, *The Next Level*, Perseus Books

FOUNDATION FOR A MARKET-LED BUSINESS

Market intelligence is the foundation and driving force for transitioning a company from one level and stage of growth to the next. Without it, businesses get stuck at the early, emerging stage. Few entrepreneurs and their management teams have had the task, not to mention the job description, of a market research specialist. Market research is key to creating the vital information and intelligence needed to devise and evolve the "brand and product positioning strategies" for the business. A strong brand positioning is a company's primary source of growth and value. Quite literally, it is the value seen by customers in a business, it opens doors for sales and pulls business from the marketplace.

MARKETING AUDIT AND ANALYSIS

Market research is the key to determining each of the four legs of the brand position stool:

1. Definition of the target audience, i.e. an "attractive market"
2. Value proposition and unique benefits on offer
3. Point of difference versus the competition
4. Strong reason to believe why you can claim to be unique and different.

It is an external focus that always avoids asking, "What do we think?" Instead, it continuously asks, "What do customers think?" "What are our competitors doing?" "What's happening in our market environment that will impact our business?"

Figure 2.2: *Market Intelligence Foundation for Marketing Planning*

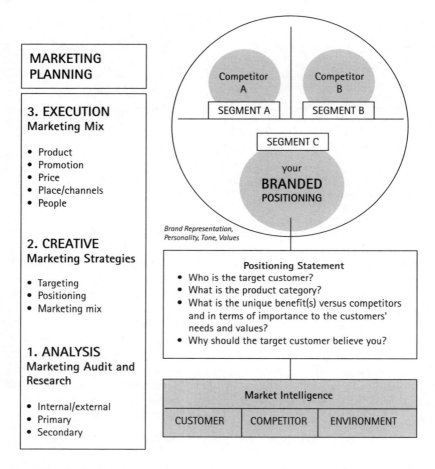

In marketing planning, this is the foundation marketing audit and analysis process. The objective of marketing audit and analysis is to create a strong brand position and strategy for the business. To provide these, research will span the company, customers, competitors and marketing environment and, as the business grows, will generate intelligence for decision making in five key areas:

1. Segmentation and targeting markets
2. Brand position (against those of competitors)
3. Product development
4. Marketing channels and communications (including the role and deployment of sales)
5. Customer satisfaction.

Research Process

Figure 2.3: *Market Research Steps*

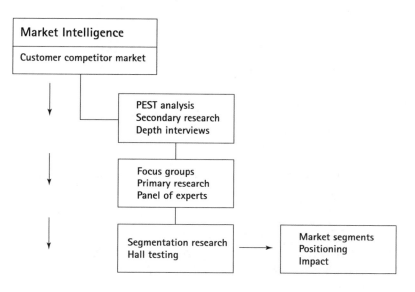

It Starts with Secondary Market Research

Secondary research is where market research usually begins and continues 24/7. It covers all available information on the industry sector, the competitors and profile information on customers and customer types. It provides good direction for specific areas of enquiry in primary research. All businesses need to know key information about their marketing environment (PEST Trend Analysis), competitors and target buyers.

External secondary market research can provide intelligence on:

- Total market size in local and international areas
- Major competitors by category
- Target buyer profile information
- Issues that impact or will impact on the market
- Trends that will change/shape the market going forward.

Speaking the Customer's Language

Understanding a target business customer's plans and financials is key to how you sell your product. If your product is irrelevant or not properly positioned to their plans and fails to address their financials, then your selling activities will be fruitless and costly. In the US, for example, good information on both plans and financials for companies is available free of charge from www.freeedgar.com. SEC Report filings such as 10-Qs are issued quarterly for public companies and contain their financial results and significant changes/events. Report 10-K is their annual report and outlook for the future. By accessing these reports for targeted customers (and their key competitors), considerable insight can be built on a target company's financial position and strategy and put to very effective use in your product positioning and sales process.

Sources of Information
Common online and people sources of external information on local and overseas markets include:

- Trade associations/industry groupings, such as the world Chamber Network (www.worldchambers.com) and the Japanese Institute for International Trade (www.jetro.go.jp)
- Editorial staff of trade publications
- Industry publications and databases – Business Alert – US (www.tdctrade.com), Business ASEAN (www.aseansec.org) Latin American Economy and Business (www.latinnews.com) and Enterprise Europe (www.europa.eu.int)
- Government agencies and information databases, such as Enterprise Ireland (www.enterprise-ireland.com) and the International Trade Centre (www.intracen.org)
- Thomas Register of American Manufacturers, sourcebook of American and Canadian manufacturers
- ACNielsen (tracks retail sales movement to consumers)
- Lexis/Nexis company and industry reports
- Bizminer.com
- Freeedgar.com
- FISonline and S&P industry surveys have industry and product category reports
- Invisibleweb.com, a database/archive/search engine site to research companies, industries and business publications
- Companysleuth.com monitors companies for free
- AskeLibrary.com to source newspaper/magazine articles and references to your search topic
- Marketresearch.com, a collection of publications from more than 350 leading research firms
- For small private company/competitor information, the Dow Jones Million Dollar Database can yield some basic info and an SIC Industry Code. This in turn can be used to identify other companies in the industry
- TSCentral.com for industry trade/expos
- Industry commentators and experts

- Industry suppliers and current domestic customers
- Former/retired staff of a leading company
- Industry analysts.

Internal secondary market research can provide important *marketing environment* information on an ongoing basis covering:

- Political and regulatory developments
- Economic and fiscal developments
- Social and cultural developments
- Technological developments, innovation and adoption
- Competitor activity.

A common way to capture this information is to allocate the task to a staff member, preferably across your organisation functions, to build the external focus of the business. Sources of PEST and competitor information will include:

- Newspapers
- Business periodicals
- Government agencies
- Websites of government agencies, industry associations, competitors
- News clipping service.

Template 1: *PEST Analysis for Market Drivers and Market Strategy*

PEST Analysis: Identify trends and issues that will shape and drive the market

Type of Change	Nature of Change	Impact/Implication
Political	Media Commentary	Fostering deep consumer concern and distrust of providers
Economic	etc.	etc.

Market Driver	Key Success Factor	Strategy
Consumer Power	Brand	Position as trustworthy
etc.	etc.	etc.

Primary Market Research

Primary market research is about devising and carrying out original/bespoke research covering specific issues and questions (around the why and how of customer buying) and it comes in two broad forms: qualitative and quantitative.

Qualitative research seeks to obtain many subjective reactions from a limited number of test subjects. Companies typically use this for:

- Learning consumer language for incorporation into marketing communications
- Buyer response to new products
- Buyer evaluation of advertising, packaging and brand positioning
- Buyer perceptions of products and category suppliers
- Buyer decision criteria and process
- Generating new ideas as part of a brainstorming process.

Quantitative research seeks to obtain reactions from many test subjects to a limited number of questions. Companies use this for:

- Buyer segmentation and clustering
- Effects of pricing movements on buyer purchase intent
- Consumer acceptance of new product, repeat buying and loyalty
- Effect of package design
- Customer satisfaction, evaluation/moment of truth criteria and rankings
- Advertising research – to monitor the communication impact (yours and a competitor) in terms of awareness, change opinions and motivate buying action.

There are four main measures of advertising:

1. Brand awareness
2. Advertising recall
3. Brand image
4. Copy testing.

Good quantitative research requires a well-designed questionnaire. Having regard to the decisions to be made and learning from the depth interviews/focus groups, the questions should be based on good common sense and good communication practices. At least 100 test respondents should be selected to have a 68 per cent to 95 per cent confidence level in predictability of test results.

Figure 2.4: *Why Consumers Buy Brands*

Consumers buy brands to satisfy a myriad of functional and emotional needs ...

To ... make money ... attract praise ... possess beauty ... be more comfortable ... work easier ... save time ... avoid pain ... be superior ... impulse ... be popular ... express love ... look younger ...

... knowing the "functional" need is often not enough.

Typical research practice would be to use qualitative research first (depth interview and focus groups) to evaluate a product/positioning/prototype idea amongst target buyer types. It would also be used to understand target group attitudes/beliefs. Having evaluated and tested the product/positioning/prototype (and attitude/belief set of a group), you should follow up with the questionnaire for quantitative research for "real-world" response. This would incorporate attitude/belief statements as segmentation research.

Figure 2.5: *How Consumers Buy Brands*

Research and Understand the Buying Process and the Best Sales Process Will Follow ...

Customer	Intermediary
1. Problem Recognition	**1. Product**
Customer becomes aware they have a need. What stimulates/triggers this?	Does the provider have the right type of product to meet customer requirements?
2. Information Search	Does the product have features that add value?
Memory search. Friends/word of mouth referrals/other sources. Now has the "consideration set".	Is the product well supported by good administration/back up?
3. Evaluation of Alternatives	If yes ...
Criteria for evaluating choices.	**2. Price**

Features wanted/not wanted. Ranking and prioritising.

4. Purchase Decision

Choose buying preference – product, package, store, method of purchase, etc.

5. Purchase Action

May differ from decision – time lapse, product availability.

6. Post–Purchase Evaluation

Cognitive dissonance. Right decision?

7. Distant Post–Purchase

Desire for relationship, frequency, method.

Is the product good value for money?

How does price compare with other companies?

If favourable ...

3. Personal

How well do I know and trust my contact in the provider?

Will he/she add value to my business with advice and support?

Is he/she "on my side"?

Is he/she authoritative in the provider organisation?

Do I owe him/her a favour?

MARKET SEGMENTATION

Market segmentation is the process of:

- Identifying groups of customers with similar needs and purchasing behaviour and allocating them to market segments
- Selecting the market segments to target, based on their relative market attractiveness
- Determining how to position new products to appeal to these target market segments
- And finally creating marketing-mix programmes to promote the products with the desired brand positioning.

Segmentation Process

Identify Customer Groups

Typically, an entrepreneurial company will start in segmentation terms by targeting market segments, as in a product category and/or broad geographical market. Initial segmentation tends to be by way of accepted classifications and/or customer purchase or usage of the product category.

Template 2: *Market Segmentation*

1. Identify groups of customers by need, buying process, response

2. Select market segments to target, having regard to competitive advantage

3. Position new products to appeal to target market segments

4. Create "marketing mix" to reach and communicate the desired brand positioning for these market segments

These will include recognised industry classifications and basic demographics (such as age, gender, etc.). Low-hanging fruit is another initial segmentation done by early stage entrepreneurs.

The risk in relying on an ongoing basis on this type of segmentation is that markets are dynamic and the segmentation may not hold true. A miss-segmented market is often worse for the entrepreneur than simply trying a mass-market approach. Another issue to contend with is the fact that price competition can easily overcome a segmentation strategy when there is little perceived difference between offerings and suppliers in a product category. A sustainable segmentation requires real differences being identified and exploited.

As the venture progresses, a *base-line segmentation study* will be done to position the business for rapid growth through new product and customer markets. Segments generated by this quantitative research technique are identified by aggregating groups of buyers who respond similarly to a set of *Basis Questions* and *Descriptor/Attitude Questions*.

Example 2.1: *Base-Line Segmentation Study for a Financial Services Company*

Segmentation Bases	Attitudes	Life Stage
	Socio-economic	Gender

Current Situation	Product Ownership	Satisfaction

Channels and Communication	Media Consumption	Preferred Contact Methods/Points

Cost Drivers	Employment Status	Smoker Status

Product Assessment	Perceived Needs by Product Category
	Reaction to Branded/New Product Concepts

Basis questions and variables used in quantitative segmentation research will typically probe the following three areas:

1. **Key customer needs.** Which key customer needs can be used to help group customers with similar needs together? Identify an important need that customers do not perceive other suppliers as meeting and then develop an innovative solution to meet that need.

Example 2.2: *Attitudinal Statements that were Asked in a Financial Services Segmentation Survey*

Statement	Agree	Agree Somewhat	Neither	Disagree	Disagree Somewhat
I generally feel confident when it comes to making decisions about financial products	☐	☐	☐	☐	☐

I worry about being sold financial products that I really do not need

☐ ☐ ☐ ☐ ☐

I would like to deal with a financial services company that sends me information on my products at least once a year

☐ ☐ ☐ ☐ ☐

2. **The customer's buying process, decision-making criteria and levels of brand loyalty.** Customer loyalty and switching dispensation are strong behaviour bases.

Example 2.3: *Buying Process Questions that were Asked in a Financial Services Segmentation Survey*

Buying Process	Options
How and from whom would you like to receive information/advice about financial products?	• Company rep calling at home • Contacting company and requesting a visit from a rep • Contacting company and receiving the information by phone • Visit branch office • From my employer, etc.
How do you like to buy different types of financial products?	Etc.
What time of day is most convenient for you to make phone calls in relation to buying financial products?	Etc.

3. **Marketing communication.** Consumers can be affected in differing ways by the marketing environment – for example, they may be strongly resistant and averse to cold calling – and these differences can be used to group like-responding consumer groups.

Example 2.4: *Questions from a Financial Services Segmentation Survey*

Marketing Environment

Which television station do you watch most?
Which radio station do you listen to most?
Do you have a personal computer?
Which daily newspaper do you read most?
Which magazines do you read most?

It is useful to group possible segmentation bases for business2business (B2B) and consumer markets into *identification bases/questions*, which can identify segments by product requirements, for example, and *response/attitudinal bases/questions*, which can be more powerful (attitudinal can lead to segmentations by purchasing behaviour, relationship requirements, brand influence and communications).

Identification Bases
In B2B markets, identification bases can include organisational demographics such as:

- Size of companies
- Growth rates
- Location
- Classification codes
- Location.

Consumer markets can be similarly segmented on these two broad identification bases, for example:

- Demographics
- Location
- Life stage
- Socio-economic characteristics
- Product usage.

Response Profile Bases
Response bases underlie why a customer buys a particular product and how a customer goes about buying a product. In the case of B2B, it is about the company's approach to doing business. For the B2B sector, response bases might be:

- Buying processes
- Distinctive business growth strategies of the company
- Distinctive business competencies.

For consumer markets, response bases might include:

- Brand loyalty
- Benefits sought/desired
- Brand perceptions
- Attitudes
- Motivation
- Lifestyle
- Purchase behaviour
- Purchase occasion.

Descriptor/Attitude Responses

Managers need *descriptors* of the segment for use in identifying the segment members for targeting purposes and an understanding of the process by which the segment members make their product choices and the buying criteria they use in selecting the bought product. A good way to start is with the customer buying process or the customer response profile (why and how). When a specific buying/response need is identified for a particular customer, they need to be clustered in some way – end-user industry or demographic.

Example 2.5: *Customer Clusters in Retail Financial Services Market*

Cluster Descriptor	Market Size	Key Attitudinal Characteristics	Channel Choice
Financially astute	20%	Confident financial product buyers interested in a relationship with a provider	At company offices Not at home
Keen learners	19%	Unconfident product buyers interested in a relationship with a provider	Choice of access channels required
Hand holder	19%	Unconfident product buyers interested in a relationship with a provider	Appointment at home or office

Target Market Selection/Market Attractiveness

Michael Porter's (1980) *competitive forces* model provides a useful framework for assessing segment attractiveness. Porter argues that the profit potential of an industry or market depends on the collective strength or otherwise of six market forces – direct competitors, customers, suppliers, potential entrants and substitute products. If, collectively, the forces are strong, then it will have a negative impact on the profit potential of the market segment. In technology-intensive industries, complementors are the sixth market force – they make a customer value your product more than you could on a stand-alone basis. Figure 2.6 below sets out some of the factors determining whether these six market forces will have a negative impact on market attractiveness.

Figure 2.6: *Assessing Market Attractiveness*

Customers	Competitors
Concentrated and purchase in large volumes Standardised product Product is a significant cost component Product does not affect quality Product does not save money	Competitors are numerous and equal in size Slow market growth Products are undifferentiated Capacity increments are large Exit barriers are high
Potential Entrants	Substitutes
Company product is not differentiated Capital requirement for entry is low No cost disadvantage for a new entrant Entrants have access to distribution	Substitutes have improved price /performance Substitutes are produced by profitable firms
Complementors	Suppliers
Strong complementary products are not available and are needed Only one or two sources for key complementary products	Few suppliers of key inputs Supplier has credible threat of forward integration

Source: Derived from Figure 3.3, "Market Forces at One Level in the Market Chain", in Adrian Ryans, Roger More, Donald Barclay, Terry Deutscher (2000) Winning Market Leadership, Strategic Market Planning for Technology-Driven Businesses, John Wiley & Sons Canada, Ltd

Product and Brand Positioning, and Marketing Communications

Once the key customer groups are "clustered" (as in the Figure 2.5, 58 per cent of customers were "interested in an ongoing relationship" with the financial services provider) and their attractiveness is assessed, detailed product and corporate brand positionings are devised. When the positioning messages are developed, tailored marketing communications programmes are created to get these positioning messages to the right target clusters.

Example 2.6: *Brand/Product Positioning and Marketing Communications for One of the Financial Services Customer Clusters/Market Segment – Keen Learners*

Customer profile	Unconfident product buyer
	Interested in a relationship
	Interested in learning more
	Prepared to take risks
	Likely to be loyal
Key customer needs	Wants a relationship and ongoing dialogue
	Wants to understand their options
	Wants a swift and simple sales process
Desired buying process	Wants a choice of access channels
	Swift and simple
Positioning for sales process	Offer information and access to advice through direct mail
	Facilitate appointment by customer
	Follow-up step with adviser
	Clear and simple information to be provided at detail level decided by the customer
Positioning for service/ relationship management	Regular personalised and ongoing contact
	Call centre to support
	Free-phone advice line
	Annual review (without pressure)
Positioning advantages versus competitors	Free information service to customer
	Depth and range of advice given
	Sales process, as desired by the customer (not the provider)

Marketing communication objectives	Establish and create awareness of the new positioning Build brand image Influence purchase process – encourage contact
Key marketing communications messages	Real two-way relationship, based on listening to what is needed

CUSTOMER SATISFACTION

There is no better way of measuring customer satisfaction in the customer segments that are key to the business going forward than asking the customers directly for their evaluation criteria of what is important to them. There is no benefit in measuring what the business *thinks* is important to the customer. Ascertain from customers what their key assessment criteria are and then measure how the business performs on those criteria. A questionnaire is the most common technique for such measurement and its content/areas of survey should be co-developed with customers.

Questionnaire

Keep it short and easy to complete. It should not be ambiguous and the customer should spend no more than fifteen minutes doing it. Cover no more than ten to fifteen parameters in the questionnaire, ones that are most important to the customer. Include key questions such as

- Would you buy again?
- Would you buy our other products?
- Would you recommend it to a friend?
- How can we serve you better? (Open ended)

Questionnaires can be done regularly by mail, with a 10–15 per cent response rate, by telephone and in specially convened customer focus groups, clinics and panels. Using a third party is best and will solicit more feedback from the customers.

Include former customers to get their perspectives and non-customers to get knowledge of your competitors.

On an ongoing basis, create a facility or process for your staff with frequent customer contact (sales, service, accounts) to capture open-ended feedback. This can help inform on new areas of customer satisfaction enquiry.

Using a five-point scale

- 1= very dissatisfied
- 2= dissatisfied
- 3= neutral
- 4= satisfied
- 5= very satisfied

the 5s are the only group not likely to defect. Adding the 4s and 5s together is not the general measure of overall customer satisfaction.

Summary

Entrepreneurs who pay continuous close attention to customers, competitors and their marketing environment – by systematically gathering and analysing key information – are better placed to make the winning marketing decisions in each of the three stages of growth. In Chapter 3, the four key areas of marketing decision making are reviewed in detail for the first growth stage – the start up/emerging growth stage.

Chapter 3

Marketing Gearbox: Decisions for Stage One Growth/Start Up and Emerging

INTRODUCTION

In this chapter, we focus on stage one, the start up and emerging growth stage, during which the venture is all about its new product and "pushing" activities – promotions, PR and personal selling – to reach and convince the initial market segments to buy the product. These initial buyers are the "low-hanging fruit" necessary to generate initial revenues and references for other buyers to buy with confidence. Initial brand build work must also be done during this stage to lead the venture into the next stage – rapid growth.

START UP AND EMERGING STAGE OVERVIEW

Company Characteristics

The earliest phase of the entrepreneurial enterprise – typically the first three to five years after establishment – is driven by the imperative of making sales. Without enough sales, there's no survival. Activities are constrained by limited financial resources. The market is approached on a chaotic, random and disorganised way initially. Low-hanging fruit is the objective.

Ingenuity substitutes for capital resources. Flexibility with an absence of policy on "how things are done" generates the ingenuity and creativity. Often, the formal business plan (for seed/first round funding such as has been gained) is irrelevant to the reality. New opportunities emerge and original market and product concepts can change significantly.

Company Goals

- Launch new product that is "different"
- Capture initial customer accounts and commercialise
- Get revenues flowing in, to fund sales push

Marketing Objectives

- Adoption of new product amongst early adopter/innovator customers/segments
- Securing initial early majority customers starts to build trust in company through brand

Communication Strategies

- Create awareness and interest among innovators and early adopters

Communication Media

- Publicity
- Personal selling
- Advertising
- Promotions

* * *

In the early start up/emerging stage of the venture, resource, time and financial constraints limit what can be done in the four key marketing areas – market intelligence, brand positioning, channels and communications. However, concentration of effort wholly on product and push activities will undermine successful transition into the rapid growth and next level stages of growth. Product and push must therefore be accompanied by some key groundwork in the four marketing areas as well.

MARKET INTELLIGENCE

Market research is the key to determining each of the four legs of the brand-positioning stool:

1. Who is your target customer?
2. What is the product category?
3. What is the unique benefit versus competitors, having regard to the customer's key buying needs?
4. Why should the target customer believe you?

Market Intelligence Methods

Start using external and internal secondary research immediately.

Secondary research: using free databases/sources to identify competitor companies, branded positioning(s), customer types and needs and market size. A good deal of secondary internal and external research can be done, inexpensively, using the sources identified in Chapter 2.

External secondary market research can be used to provide:

- Total market size
- Major competitors by category
- Target buyer profile information
- Issues that impact or will impact on the market
- Trends that will change/shape the market going forward.

Internal secondary market research will be used to provide important marketing environment information on an ongoing basis covering:

- Political and regulatory developments
- Economic and fiscal developments
- Social and cultural developments
- Technological developments, innovation and adoption
- Competitor activity.

What is this market intelligence telling you about the innovators and early adopters of your initial product offer? Who will be the "early majority" customers? What "partners" in the marketplace can help you cross the "chasm" from one group to the other?

Use *primary research* methods to probe target buyers for brand, product and buying process information. Methods to use:

- **Surveys:** a simple survey card made available at your premises, at exhibitions and in customer mailings. Include the website address and ask questions at the end of customer phone calls.

- **Depth interviews:** running one-to-one interviews over 20 to 30 minutes with individual buyers and non-buyers can help to clarify and define the agenda of investigation for a number of focus groups consisting of targets.

- **Focus groups:** six to ten individuals in round-table interactive discussion, with a clear definition of what you are trying to understand. They are usually moderated by a third party and run in a series of pairs. Time duration will be 2 to 2 $^{1}/_{2}$ hours. Focus is on attitudes and beliefs, not behaviour. Advantages are:

- Learn consumer language around categories, brands and services
- Structure assumptions/hypotheses regarding attitudes and beliefs
- Develop assumptions/hypotheses regarding reactions to a new product or service.

Template 3: *Market Research Process*

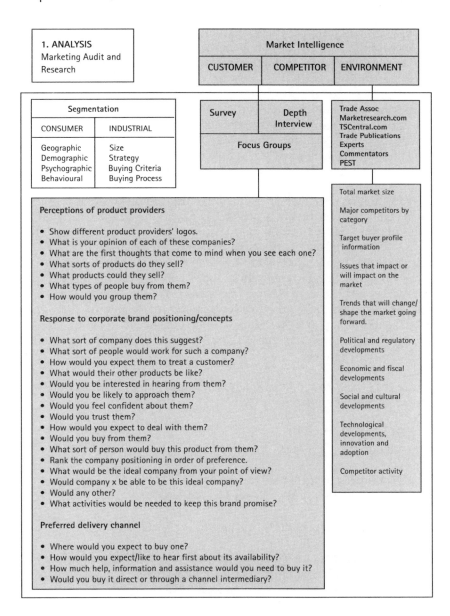

Start Building a Market Intelligence Process into the Business

Embrace the external market-driven focus from this early stage in the business and anticipate investing in a competent, strategic marketing function. Start with a marketing executive whose primary task is to concentrate on sourcing and developing market intelligence for the emerging senior management team. The CEO/entrepreneur should wear the marketing leadership hat and foster the acquisition of the customer/competitor/environment intelligence, ensuring it is factored into decision making by the top team. (As the business moves into rapid growth stage, recruit a senior level marketer to lead/execute the key marketing processes and ultimately deliver the annual marketing planning process as a top team member.)

Separate sales and marketing from the beginning. Although a strong sales organisation is important and necessary for growing companies, a real and common constraint to growth is marketplace change. Working harder and better at sales is not going to be effective in a market that shifted from an innovator/early adopter to an early majority one or in a new direction. Marketing is a key "directional" function that should be gathering market intelligence from the start. When marketing is done well, it happens long before a product is made or a market is entered – and it continues long after the sale.

Significant investment in systematic research practices will have to await the lesser financial constraints in rapid growth stage.

Consolidating the gathering and analysis of market intelligence – to align market realities with strategic decision making – will be done in the rapid growth stage by the senior level marketer as part of the annual marketing planning process. Market intelligence will then be used to generate new strategies for growth and to innovate positioning, product and marketing channels

Example 3.1: *Focus Group Research on Corporate Brand/New Product for a Financial Services Company*

---

1. Introduction

- Ask attendees to introduce themselves
- What brands do you feel closest to and why?

2. Product Ownership and Perceptions

- Probe ownership of product x type and other category products
- Probe companies they have had experience of
- Which product x types have you heard of?

- Probe full list to gauge understanding of products available
- What product x's do you own?
- What was the trigger to purchase?
- What others did you consider?
- What are your main reasons for having a product x?
- Are certain product x's more suitable/better than others to meet your objectives?
- What were the main things you were looking for when you bought the product?
- From whom did you buy it?
- Why?
- How did you go about buying it?
- What influenced you, positively and negatively?
- Have you or anyone you know had any problems with it?

3. Responses to a New Product Concept

- Do you understand the product description?
- What do you like/dislike about it?
- What are the main benefits?
- Is it relevant to your needs?
- Does it appeal?
- Who might want it?
- How could it be improved?
- Could company brand positioning offer this product?
- If you were to remix the product features for the most appealing, what would you select and why?
- For those who do not have a product x type, would this make you buy one?

4. Current Relationships with Providers and Ideal Relationships

- How would you describe your relationship with your current provider?
- Do you think they provide good service?
- What do you expect versus what they deliver?
- What is a good relationship? And a bad one?
- How much contact do you want after purchase?
- Would you want to hear about new products?

MARKET SEGMENTATION

An entrepreneur has to adopt either a mass-market strategy or a market-segmentation strategy. There is no in-between. In positioning a product, a target audience for the product must be identified and defined. This is the role of market segmentation.

Initial Segmentation for this Stage

Initial market segmentation for start up and emerging stage entrepreneurs is usually around defining customer groups according to generally accepted classifications. These are typically around variations in customer purchase or usage of the product category. This may be a recognised industrial classification, geographical region or basic demographic descriptors such as gender, age or income. These identification bases do not lend themselves to gaining a sustainable competitive advantage – many competitors will address the market using these identification methods for target customer groups. Innovative new products can make up for this in the short term and early emerging stage.

Competitive advantage and differentiation will often come from looking for response bases to identify an uncovered market segment and these in turn will emerge from three areas of enquiry:

1. Customer needs that are not met (or unsatisfactorily met) by other competitors
2. Desired customer buying process, decision-making process requirements and brand loyalty propensity
3. Response and behaviour in relation to marketing communications and environment.

During the emerging stage, begin asking questions of customers and target customers and building up market intelligence in these four areas:

1. Perceptions of product providers, their brands and loyalty to them
2. Current relationships with providers and desired ideal relationships
3. Product ownership, needs and perceptions of benefits, gaps and opportunities
4. Preferred awareness, buying and delivery channels.

This will help identify innovator/early adopter and early majority customer types and will inform the full focus-group/depth-interview research and subsequent base-line segmentation research to be done for powering the rapid growth stage of development and equipping the business to jump to the next level of growth.

CORPORATE BRAND POSITIONING

For most start up and emerging entrepreneurs, the business is primarily a new product-led venture. Branding strategy and decisions will be the key to success or failure for new entrants to a marketplace and/or as would-be providers of a radical new product, which requires change and trust on the part of the buyers.

Brand: The Most Important Business Strategy

From start up to exit and value realisation, brand is the entrepreneur's most important business strategy. It facilitates successful market entry at the start up stage, it provides the mechanism and lever for structuring the business in the rapid growth stage and it becomes the value to be realised by the entrepreneur at the next level stage – and all through the venture's development growth path it is a beacon for its corporate governance.

Branding starts as the business's compelling value proposition for the buyer (the brand position), i.e. it captures the buyer's attention and loyalty by filling an unmet or unsatisfied need. It becomes the business's most valuable asset, as the brand position and what it stands for are used as the driving force and framework for all management, financial, operational and planning decision making in the organisation. Significant value is attributed to this clarity of focus, strategy and organisational structuring by the investment community. Brand governance underpins best practice corporate governance – both are critically concerned with reputation.

From the Start ...

Confidence and trust are the two powerful underlying drivers for consumers when they make their buying considerations, selections and decisions. Having the greatest product, the lowest price and the fastest service will not cut it with the buyer if they do not trust or have confidence in you. In today's cluttered marketplace, with a myriad of providers all sending out their audio and visual messages, buyers are not going to go out of their way looking for you and what you have to offer. In today's fast-paced, complex, time-is-money society, buyers are not going to waste their precious time looking for ways to make themselves trust you or have confidence in you. Only those providers that stand out in the marketplace, that are intrinsically striking and that can create an indelible, favourable impression on the buyer are included in the small number of companies that a buyer will first consider to meet their buying need (known as their "consideration set").

Brands are the antidote to buyer uncertainty and lack of trust and confidence. Brands have been used to grow businesses successfully, because buyers want them and use them to make confident buying decisions. Brands also grow businesses because they protect a business's reputation and credibility in the marketplace.

Successful businesses set up and organise themselves around a distinctive value proposition (or brand position) for the buyer. This is where branding starts – a clear point of view on what the business is about, what its differentiated value proposition to the buyer is and how it will sustain this competitive advantage. Visual and verbal elements of the branding, from elements such as name and logo to corporate literature, web and sales staff, symbolise that differentiated value proposition (brand position) and work to lodge it firmly and indelibly in the buyer's mindset.

... To Exit and Value Realisation

Successful brands always deliver on their value proposition. The promise and expectation of the brand position must become the buyer's experience in reality every time. To achieve this consistently, businesses use their brand position as the central organisation mission and as the management lever to guide decision making on all aspects of and interfaces with their buyers – all products, promotions, services and operations are developed and organised to continually deliver the brand position. Brands thereby become the business's most stable and sustainable asset. This is the entrepreneur's value realisation on exit. If the brand continues to deliver its value proposition, if it continues to innovate and add value to it, then buyers will continue to buy it, respect it and even come to love it! Brands live on, long after an entrepreneur exits and management teams move on.

Start Up and Emerging Stage Branding Steps

In the start up/emerging stage, the focus is necessarily on positioning the new venture's first products and branding work that can be carried through into the next growth stage, with minimal brand value or equity being lost as a result of, for example, changing the business name.

There are three pieces of essential branding work to be done during the start up/emerging stage.

1. Create and define the brand/product position statement
2. Create and communicate the brand personality for that position
3. Be careful and singular about the company you keep.

Brand/Product Position Statement

A brand or product position (also known as value proposition) statement is the tight, researched and documented statement of:

- Who is the target customer?
- What is the product category? What does it do or replace?
- What is the unique customer benefit versus the competition – not features?

- *Why* should the target customers believe you? What proof is there?

This statement of the venture's attractive, compelling offer is the key input into defining what your business is and what you stand for. It also informs all key elements of the brand personality. The company name is the most important element of a brand personality and its visual distinction in the marketplace. The name provides a universal reference point through language and it is the one element of the brand personality that has to be got right and should never change thereafter.

If the research and development work is not done to create the four-point position statement, then the company name will probably not be as distinctive as it should be in the target market and the probability of having to change it in the future increases. This represents a serious and significant value loss to the business.

Brand Personality

Brand personality is the sum of all visual and verbal elements used to make the brand position distinctive and appealing in the marketplace. These elements are:

- Name
- Logo
- Letters
- Numbers
- Symbols
- Signature
- Shapes
- Slogan
- Colour
- Typeface
- Publicity
- Promotional materials
- Promotions
- Advertising
- Packaging
- Web
- Sales staff
- Service staff
- Stories/cause.

Which Distinctive Elements?

Consumers and businesses are bombarded daily with promotional and advertising noise; they receive hundreds of textual and auditory messages from morning until night, 24/7 and 365 days a year. To cut through this clutter, the brand personality must be carried through all interface and communication channels with the customer systematically and consistently. This consistent representation is critical and will lead to a point where your target audience will know who you are, what you offer and the value they will experience with you repeatedly.

Philip Kotler (2001) identifies strong brand personalities as typically having

- an owned word
- a slogan
- a colour
- a symbol (logo)
- and a set of stories

strongly or exclusively associated with it in the market's mindset.

Brand Name

Being competent or expert, reliable and forward thinking make up the building blocks of being credible in interpersonal communications. The brand name provides the universal reference point in interpersonal communications and it should therefore draw upon these attributes for credibility in communication. The brand name should therefore convey:

- Expertise in the business you are in
- Value and uniqueness of offer benefit, worthy of trust
- Forward-thinking attributes.

The most effective name will be derived from the mission statement, which is derived from the brand position/statement and what the business stands for.

The brand name can be abstract, informative, coined (made up), descriptive or suggestive. It can also be a conventional word or a new word/spelling. It should be meaningful, real and easy to pronounce, recognise and remember. The brand name should not be difficult to explain, fabricated (numbers or initials), narrowly defined or carry a poor/inappropriate meaning in other countries. Factor in also how it will be registered on the worldwide web. In the US, for example, it is preferable to register a ".com" address, rather than an Irish ".ie" address.

Deciding the Name

Firstly, define the *brand position statement* and then articulate the *mission statement*. This mission statement should:

- Capture the essence of your business goals and underlying philosophies
- Signal what your business is about to your customers, employers, suppliers and community
- Reflect the facets of your business – range/nature of products, pricing, quality, marketplace position, growth potential, use of technology and your relationships with customers, employers, etc.

Figure 3.1: *Questions to Help you Define your Mission Statement*

---

1. Why are you in this business? What do you want for yourself, your family and your customers? Think about the spark that ignited your decision to start the business. What will keep it burning?

2. Who are your customers? What can you do for them that will enrich their lives and contribute to their success – now and in the future?

3. What image of your business do you want to convey? Customers, suppliers, employees and the public will all have perceptions of your company. How will you create the desired picture?

4. What is the nature of your products and services? What factors determine pricing and quality? Consider how these relate to the reasons for your business's existence. How will this change over time?

5. What level of service do you provide? Most companies believe they offer the "best service available", but do your customers agree? Do not be vague; define what makes your service so extraordinary

6. What roles do you and your employees play? Wise captains develop a leadership style that organises, challenges and recognises employees.

7. What kind of relationships will you maintain with suppliers? Every business is in partnership with its suppliers – when you succeed, so do they.

8. How do you differ from competitors? Many entrepreneurs forget they are pursuing the same dollars as their competitors. What do you do better, cheaper or faster than other competitors do? How can you use competitors' weaknesses to your advantage?

9. How will you use technology, capital, processes products and services to reach your goals? A description of your strategy will keep your energies focused on your goals.

10. What underlying philosophies or values guided your responses to the previous questions? Some businesses choose to list these separately. Writing them down clarifies the "why" behind your mission.

Secondly, brainstorm (review dictionaries, industry and trade magazines, etc.) to generate possible names. As a guide, the popularity of company name lengths, by number of words in its title, is:

- Two words   9%
- Three words   50%
- Four words   35%
- Five+ words   6%

A combination name can be arrived at by dividing the name up into three elements.

Figure 3.2: *Generating Combination Names*

Who? *(distinctive element)*	What? *(primary activity)*	How? *(type of organisation)*
1. Advanced	Tyre	Corporation
2.		
3.		
4.		
5.		
6.		
7.		
8.		
9.		
10.		

Narrow the possible names down to at least ten that fit your brand position/mission statement. Select the best five using criteria relevant to your business and marketing strategies (pronunciation, language translation, competitive strategy, competitor names). Complete a trademark search (and in the largest target markets) for the five names. Register the names that are not duplicated or already trademarked.

Developing the Logo
Once the name has been decided, the next decision lies in its logo representation. The logo should reflect the overall image needed by the company to convey what its business is to the target markets. Therefore, when developing the logo, it is important to work with a good design agency, ensuring the effective use of colour, font and graphics. The logo is a very important design element, being carried through all your

communication materials/media (stationery, signage, web, brochures, manuals, etc.). Logos come in two basic forms, and combinations thereof:

1. Abstract symbols – use with your company name, for example the Nike "swoosh"
2. Logo types or stylised renditions of the company name, for example Microsoft.

Figure 3.3: *Brand Logos*

- Colours are the basic visual component of your brand. Colours inspire emotional response: neutral colours communicate confidence; highly contrasting colours create energy and movement; low contrast presents subtle and quiet.
- Red is often associated with vibrancy, passion, energy, vitality and power. In design, it is the attention grabber.
- Yellow is associated with cheerfulness and when used as a background with black typeset it scores very highly in terms of reader memory retention and legibility. The human eye notices this colour combination first.
- Blue is widely held to be a calming colour. Dark blue conveys dignity.
- Green is used in design to stimulate/uplift when used in bright shades and to evoke calm and quiet when used in dark shades.
- Black is the embodiment of sophistication, giving an "expensive" message.
- Font selection has a big effect. The first and most important factor in choosing your font is readability. If your marketing is going to be mostly on the web and/or text-light in brochures etc., then you should use a sans-serif font. It is more readable in these communication media and looks more modern, flexible and dynamic. If your marketing relies on text-rich communications, then use serif fonts (such as Times New Roman). They are classic, strong and very readable.

Brand Tag Line

In less than ten words, the brand tag line provides an instant summary of the brand positioning. A way to draft the tag line is to set out briefly:

1. Our company expertise is in ... (what field or product category?)
2. We uniquely offer customers ... (what products/key benefits?)
3. We appeal most to ... (what target audience?)

Always attach the tag line to your logo.

Finally ...

When the brand name, logo and tag line are in design format, test them in the following three ways before finally deciding on the design:

1. Place the designed name/logo/tag line on stationery and business cards – does it all work?
2. Fax a letter with the name/logo/tag line design to a fax machine – how does it come out: clear or all dark and difficult to read?
3. Expand the size of the name and logo to a big poster size or even a 48-sheet outdoor poster size – how does it work? Does it lose impact?

The Company you Keep

During the start up/emerging stage, a lot can be perceived about the business by the company it keeps. Be strategic and singular in the following:

- Promoting the CEO and his/her profile in the marketplace
- Appointing members of the board of directors
- Having a panel of advisors
- The investors, first taken on/and in subsequent rounds
- Advisors (audit/assurance, financial and legal)
- The strategic marketing management team (CEO and marketing director)
- The sales management team
- Channel distributors and re-sellers
- Alliance, joint ventures and partners
- Reference customers.

Top-tier advisors to your business and business alliances can be powerful partners to help you cross the chasm from initial success in your innovator/early adopter customer base and on into your business liquidity zone in the early majority customer markets.

PRODUCT POSITIONING

Define your Position

For a business to be viable, it has to do something *as well as* its competitors; to win in a competitive market, it has to do something *better than* its competitors. Most early stage entrepreneurs are strongly product focussed and it is important at this emerging stage that time is invested to position the product carefully. A critical requirement in positioning is how it differs from competitor offerings on attributes/benefits that matter most to the target buyer.

Effective product positioning reduces the costs of ineffective marketing and selling.

Product positioning is the unique or first place your product benefits have in the minds of your target customer. There are many ways for a product to be unique and distinctive: from small pricing, packaging and service differences to significant feature, benefit and performance differences to the competitor products. In all cases, product uniqueness has to be assessed and stated in relation to the other products that the target buyer already uses, as supplied by competitors. How important the "unique" product benefits are will be determined by the impact they have on the customer's buying criteria, decisions and process.

Meaningful and valued differences in product benefits – compared to the competitors – can be created and communicated to the target buyer group via:

- Packaging
- Pricing
- Features and benefits
- Product design
- Colour
- Advertising and promotion mediums
- Public relations and media reach
- Trade events
- Sales materials
- Sales people.

Positive, attractive and motivating differences have to be created in the target customer's mind and perception. Perception is reality. Marketing creativity is the key skill-set in creating this perception. Very often marketing creativity can be a competitive differentiator.

Unique Selling Propositions (USPs)

At the start up and emerging stage, a concise definition of the product USPs is critical. This should then be used consistently and continuously in all marketing and selling activities. Several questions need to be answered to arrive at a concise description of the product USP:

- What is unique about the product versus the direct competitors?
- Of the differences, which are the most important for a buyer of this product (category)?
- Of the differences, which are not easily imitated by the competitors?
- Of the differences, which can be easily communicated and understood by the buyer?
- Of the differences, at what stage of the buying process are they most

relevant – awareness creation/attention grabbing, fostering the interest of the buyer, creating a buying desire and finally the buying action itself?

- Can a memorable message be created about these differences/USPs?
- What marketing communications and channels can be used to get the message to the target buyers?

Securing Trust in Radical New Product

Trust in a new product/technology has to be earned by the seller. Buyers will be fearful, uncertain and doubtful about buying something entirely new to them. Some categories of buyers, however, will be more willing to try a purchase. These are the early adopters and innovators. They can be courted by incorporating the following seven requirements into all marketing communications and sales process with them.

1. The new product/technology must be perceived by the buyer as being better than what they currently or previously used. Independent verification of quality, standards and benefits is essential.
2. It must be compatible with the buyer's people, processes and technology.
3. It must be easy to use: perceived complexity slows adoption.
4. It must be easy to try out. Free use, for a trial/period, improves adoption.
5. It must be easy for the buyer to see the benefits. Benefits in terms of easing or eliminating pain are more motivating for buyers and generate quicker adoption.
6. In sales push, seek out the innovator and early adopter prospective customers. These customers will be interested in buying a new product for the sake of its innovation and will work to co-develop it further for mass production and marketing.
7. Education is key to market adoption of a radical new product. Involve credible third parties to address the issues and problems that the new product solves. Invite customers to provide "testimonials" on how the product solves those problems.

New product adoption will be helped by the extent to which the business has successfully developed a credibility-based brand name and logo, symbolising expertise, future orientation and trustworthiness.

Get the Innovators and Early Adopters

Innovators (2.5 per cent) and *early adopters* (13.5 per cent) will be the critical foothold in a radical new technology or product market, typically accounting for 16 per cent of the market. In new technology or radical product innovation, the earliest adopters are the innovators. Innovators like to try out new products and ideas, they like lots of information, they read up in technical/professional journals and they do not need a final solution. They are critical to legitimising the new product and to convincing others that it works. Next come the early adopters or visionaries, who see the potential benefits that will accrue – personally and organisationally – if they aggressively use the new product to achieve competitive advantage.

Both of these groups are key targets at the start up and emerging stage of the entrepreneur's business. Use your knowledge of their characteristics and work with the innovators to demonstrate product viability and to jointly educate the early adopters.

Figure 3.4: *Early Adopters of a New Product*

Target Group	Innovators *Enthusiasts*	Early Adopters *Visionaries*
Focus	New idea/product	Breakthrough that will create advantage
Characteristics	Product knowledgeable Appreciates new ideas Likes to test new ideas Does not need final solution	Can imagine applications Willing to take risks Willing to invest to create full solution Not price sensitive
Needs	Early access to emerging idea/product Involvement in information sharing	Lots of support Wants to move quickly
Role in adoption process	Confirms viability	Helps commercialise Gives visibility

Source: Derived from Figure 4.4, "Key Characteristics, Needs and Role of Adopter Groups" in Adrian Ryans, Roger More, Donald Barclay, Terry Deutscher, Winning Market Leadership: Strategic Market Planning for Technology-Driven Businesses, John Wiley & Sons Canada Ltd, 2000

If the next stage – rapid growth – is to be achieved, the market focus will change from these innovators and early adopters and the key is to get the early majority buyers (34 per cent) on board. With this market segment comes business liquidity.

CHANNEL MANAGEMENT

When the product has been developed and it has been determined how best to "position" it in the most attractive way in the most profitable buyer segment(s), the selection and management of distribution or market channels will follow. Amongst the important aspects of channel strategy and selection is the need to provide more choice to the customer and to operate "key account management" for the top accounts, which generate the 80 per cent of revenues. Below are the range and type of channels to market, a number of which can be used to support key account management: business centres, desk-based account management, telemarketing and e-channel.

Initial Channel Choice

In broad terms, the types of distribution or market channel available include:

- Retail outlet, owned by your company or independent merchant
- Wholesale outlets of your own or those of independent distributors or brokers
- Sales force, salaried and/or commission paid
- Outsourced representatives, who will carry your product, for a commission, to the market alongside other manufacturers' products
- Servicing staff, who can identify opportunities for up-sell/on-sell/cross-sell
- Direct mail via own catalogue or marketing
- Telemarketing/contact centres through own sales force or through a contract team
- E-marketing using your own website or an industry portal
- TV and cable network home shopping channels
- SMS/mobile
- PDAs.

Initial Channel Decision

When the target market is known and the buying process and product/positioning is defined, it will become apparent as to the channel(s) by which the audience can best become aware of the positioning, realise it is relevant to them/their needs and then be convinced to purchase and become loyal customers.

Template 4: *Channel Decision Process*

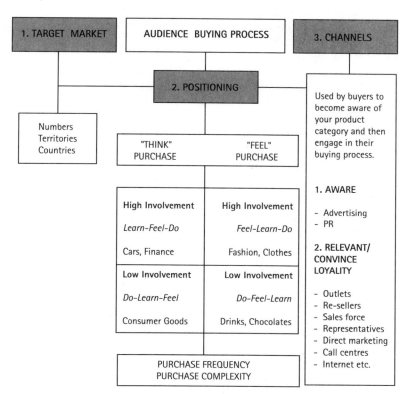

Identify the Directly Competing Competitors

The start up/emerging stage entrepreneur should focus initially on the competitors that compete directly with them for the same list of target customers in their local marketing area. Sources of information on who they are and how they distribute can be primary research (buyers) and secondary research (trade industry associations, trade suppliers, websites, newspapers/trade magazines).

Assess Strengths and Weaknesses – Opportunities and Threats

When undertaking primary research (buyers) and secondary research (industry associations, trade suppliers, websites, newspapers/trade magazines), cover the following key questions:

- What are the barriers and difficulties to entering this product category – via each distribution channel?

- How much do various distribution channels cost to enter successfully? Over what period does the cost occur?
- How have previous entrants entered the market – all segments using all channels?
- How did the existing market competitors respond – product/price /promotion/sales force?
- Are there any channel product seasonality/life cycle peculiarities?
- Are there any management, control, loyalty issues or risks associated with a particular channel?
- What is the likely frequency of referrals/volume of business levels by channel?

Match those Channels that Fit Company Resources and Product Positioning

In the start up and emerging stages, the entrepreneur has limited (time, personnel and financial) resources and it is often best to select a limited number of channels that offer:

- Greatest ease of market segment entry, against the competition
- Distribution methods and dynamics that are understood/previously experienced by your management
- Lowest cost of entry, compared to the competition
- Best fit with brand and product positioning, for example "complex" products will need dedicated sellers or re-sellers
- Least financial risk
- Strategic commitment to distribution of your product
- Likely to be permanent
- Sufficient volume potential to reach immediate and short-term revenue and profit goals
- Alternative routes to market, should one lapse or cease producing business
- Significant level of control in at least one channel to ensure you can communicate fully your product positioning (USP) and can keep the end customer knowledgeable at all times to evolve and develop that positioning.

A Channel Model

Companies are now learning to create, deploy and manage integrated channel mixes to maximise market coverage and minimise costs.

As the emerging entrepreneur business moves on to rapid growth stage, other/further channels (such as above) are added, developed and integrated. In rapid growth stage, *key account management* and *intermediary/re-seller* development will become major channel objectives. Channel strategies will be devised for competitive advantage, which may include:

- A dedicated sales force to acquire and grow key accounts
- Distributor network management to reach dispersed groups of customers and to provide local support
- Call centres to close simple sales, generate sales leads for other channels and follow up direct mail campaigns
- Internet to reach customers who want to serve themselves.

Figure 3.5: *Channel Model Illustration*

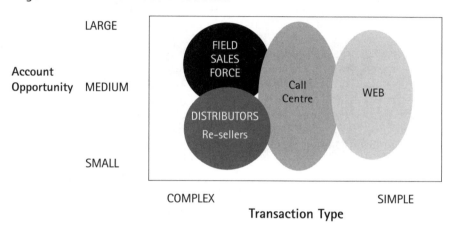

INTEGRATED MARKETING COMMUNICATIONS

Positioning Statement

The brand/product positioning statement is the heartbeat of an effective, integrated marketing communications programme. A powerful brand/product positioning (or customer value proposition) makes possible a strong brand personality – one that is visually distinctive so as to capture the target market's attention and that is significantly differentiated and relevant so as to make an indelible impression.

Everybody (sales, service operations, etc.) and every medium (product, brochure, press ad, PR, website, etc.) need to follow the positioning statement and deliver its messages to the market. The start up and emerging entrepreneur's positioning statement (how the business wishes to be seen in the market) will identify:

- The product category/business they are in
- The target audience served
- The unique benefit offered, versus competitors, that meets the customer's key needs and values

- The reasons why the target audience should believe you (the proof).

Communication Steps

There are several steps through which a product and/or brand must go in a consumer's mind before it gains acceptance. In the first step, the product/brand must capture or grab the customer's *attention*. In a cluttered world with many messages being sent through many media, every hour of every day, this is a critical and difficult communications task. What attracts and holds attention? Amongst the things that do are:

- Consumers pay attention to things that have implications or impact on their lives and their needs, values and goals
- They also pay attention to people they can relate to – people who look, act, speak or seem like them
- Rhetorical questions capture consumers' attention
- Imagery will create better brand name recall, higher brand recognition, better recognition of logos and better brand promise recall
- Consumers attend to things that are pleasant, that make them feel good
- Attractive visuals are engaging, as are familiar songs and musical pieces
- Humour can be attention grabbing, but must be related to the advert product/brand – otherwise people just remember the joke
- Consumers attend to novel things that surprise them and can be engaged by the unexpected (not new, but unusual)
- Visual design is an important element of communication. For example, the eye is always attracted to coloured elements before black and white elements, isolated elements before elements in a group and graphics before text. People in Western cultures always look at the upper left corner of a screen or ad for the most important information. Use of too many colours results in visual clutter, as does using too many fonts and over-use of italics.

In the second step, the consumer must become *aware* of the product/brand. Capturing someone's attention does not mean they will necessarily notice the brand name – this needs to be made focal. The third step involves the creation of product/brand *knowledge* – the point at which comprehension of the product/brand and what they mean becomes important. Questions about the product/brand benefits, differentiation from competitors, whom it is for and proof of delivery must be answered. The fourth step is product/brand *attitude* – persuading the consumer and building their conviction in the product's/brand's suitability for their emotional and functional needs. The final step is the purchase action.

Figure 3.6: *Communication Flows, Barriers and Accelerators*

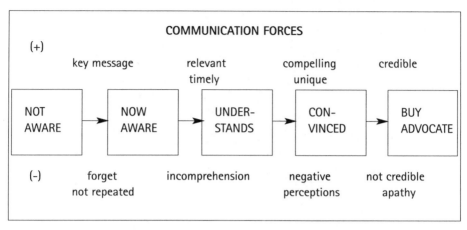

Business and Consumer Communication Differences

Marketing communications in B2B and B2C (business2customer) can be characterised as follows:

Figure 3.7: *Difference Between Consumer and Business Communications*

Marketing Communication Programme Feature	B2C	B2B
Communication context	Informal	Formal
Number of decision makers	One/few	Many
Primary tool	Advertising and sales promotion	Personal Selling
Communication content	Emotion Imagery Information	Rational Functional
Decision period	Short	Long Involved

	Limited		Wide	
Dissatisfaction impact scope	Limited		Wide	
Typical budget allocation				
• Low value product	Advertising	50%	Advertising	20%
	Publicity	10%	Publicity	10%
	Promotion	25%	Promotion	25%
	Selling	15%	Selling	25%
• High value product	Advertising	35%	Advertising	10%
	Publicity	10%	Publicity	10%
	Promotion	25%	Promotion	25%
	Selling	30%	Selling	55%

Source: Derived from Varey (2002)

Initial Communication Methods and Objectives

Where a start up and emerging entrepreneur has introduced a radical new product and is in effect creating a market space, it is useful to map the use of communication tools according to the "product life cycle" and their stages of growth.

Figure 3.8: *Communication Objectives and Tools by Stage of Growth*

	STAGES OF BUSINESS GROWTH		
	Start Up/Emerging	Rapid Growth	Next Level
	PRODUCT LIFE CYCLE		
Objectives	Introduction	Growth	Maturity	Reinvent
Marketing objectives	Help innovators and early adopters try/develop the product	Gain market share Early majority Brand position Establish channels	Strengthen market share Late majority Brand position Key accounts Product range	New markets "demand innovation"
Communication objectives	Create awareness, interest and desire among innovators and early adopters	Create brand preference Encourage wider use	Increase frequency of use	Create new markets

50

Communication strategy/ prioritised use of tools	Publicity Personal selling Advertising Promotion	Advertising Personal selling Promotion Publicity	Advertising Intermediary Promotion Publicity	Promotion

Source: Derived from Varey (2002)

Advertising

Advertising is a powerful marketing communication tool that delivers results according to the "garbage-in/garbage-out" formula of life. To get the best results, it is worth following a procedure such as the one suggested in Template 5. When the best possible advertisement has been generated by the process, the advertisement placement will need repetition and at least two other marketing communication tools to reinforce the cut-through/message-reach to the target audience (for example use of radio, e-marketing and call centre, or direct mailing and call centre).

Always be clear on the advertising campaign objectives: is it to affect attitudes towards the product/brand or is it to create sales, on foot of calls for information? Always be clear about who the target is, not just in terms of market types but also whether targets are potential buyers who are already in the market (the involved market) or whether targets have to be first "educated" about the product category/need.

Real discipline is required in selecting the best, most powerful single-selling proposition. In cluttered, busy markets, only this will work. Advertisements have perhaps three seconds to grab attention (assuming the advertising agency creative delivers the "grabber" in the ad). It then has to be compelling and involving *to hold* the audience's attention sufficiently long so they learn the next step they should take to purchase your product. Comparing and differentiating the single-selling proposition benefits to a competitor's or to the customer's current (unhappy) state can be a very powerful advertising communication.

With a really strong positioning (selling proposition), branding delivers insulation against a competitor stealing that position in the market. It is very important therefore to take the results of the corporate brand development work (Chapter 4, Template 15, Corporate Brand Positioning Development Process) and work with the advertising agency creative team to devise the distinctive brand personality that "owns" the brand/product position.

Template 5: *Advertising Campaign Planning Process*

ADVERTISING
Pro-forma/Procedure

Advertising Campaign Specification for:

1.   Advertising Campaign Objectives:

_____
_____
_____
_____
_____
_____
_____
_____

Indirect ⟵——————————————————————————————⟶ Direct
effect on   effect on
sales   ☐   ☐   ☐   ☐   ☐   ☐   sales

| 1. Reinforce attitudes (reinforce existing behaviours) | 2. Modify attitudes (change future existing behaviour) | 3. Recall satisfaction (reinforce needs behaviours) | 4. Relate brand to own | 5. Seek info | 6.Buy |

---

2. Audience Being Targeted: ☐ **Active involved consumers**

☐ **Inactive, uninvolved potential future consumers**

_____
_____
_____
_____
_____
_____
_____

Low involvement
in product ⟵——————————————————————————————⟶ High involvement
category/   in product
low interest in   category/
advertising   high interest in
                                                                                advertising

☐   ☐   ☐   ☐   ☐

| 1. No perceived need for product category | 2. Recognition of latent product need | 3. Passive consideration of product need | 4. Search/review of product choices | 5. Purchase product |

Communication Message(s)	Awareness	Interest	Information/advice	Evaluation	Action

---

3. The Single-Minded Selling Proposition:

_____
_____
_____
_____
_____
_____

What Stage of the Buying Process are we Influencing?

Stage   Proposition

Stage	Proposition
No Perceived Need	
Need Recognition	
Interest	
How to Buy Who From	
Evaluation	
Purchase	

4. What Is Different about the Proposition?

_____
_____
_____
_____
_____
_____
_____

5. Budget, Media Specifications:

Total budget (include VAT) € ———— Production € ——— Media € ————

BTL   € ———

_____
_____
_____
_____

Brand Personality	Brand Creative	Brand Values
☐ (Description)	☐ (Description)	☐ (Description)
☐	☐	☐
☐	☐	☐
☐	☐	☐
☐	☐	☐
☐	☐	☐
☐	☐	☐
☐	☐	☐

* * *

For start up and emerging stage entrepreneurs, the principal marketing communication tools used will be their corporate/product brochure, attending exhibitions/trade shows and expos, organising open days, generating and promoting case studies, testimonials and referrals, generating and using PR/publicity to create credibility, using direct marketing to generate leads and personal selling. Hereunder are checklists for ensuring success for each.

Corporate/Product Brochures

Three Golden Rules

Three golden rules define the effective use of brochures to communicate the positioning, build the brand, generate sales and foster client loyalty.

1. All brochures should be integrated within and be a planned part of an overall marketing and sales campaign.

    - Brochures work best and more effectively when they are used as part of a comprehensive, single-selling message campaign, for example when mailed during a print or radio advertising campaign or when used at an exhibition by staff on the stand.
    - In the absence of other promotional support in a campaign, brochures should only be used if staff are following up each mailing with an individual phone call.
    - Brochure mailings without follow-up phone-calls are not effective.

2. There must be a clear view of the job a brochure has to do and at what stage in the selling cycle it is to operate.

    - There are three generic types of brochure and each only operates effectively at the right stage of the selling cycle. These are:

i. **Sales brochure:** the purpose of this brochure is to grab attention, create awareness, generate interest and facilitate a response from the recipient. Successful sales brochures deliver the "hook" or the attractive proposition to the recipient and "talk" like a catchy advertisement. It is not a detailed information provider or a response device.

ii. **Information brochure:** this type of brochure operates at a very different stage of the selling cycle and therefore it sells in a way that the sales brochure does not. The information brochure is needed at the coal face of the buying decision: in a clear, uncluttered, gimmick-free, no-sales-copy way, it provides the information that the recipient needs to address any queries and confirm the reasons to buy. It is a factual brochure.

iii. **Corporate brochure:** the corporate brochure promotes the "provider" and not the products of the provider. Only brief details of product are included – if at all – and typical content will be company history and case/client histories. Text and imagery must be consistent with the corporate brand, brand promise and brand values. It is factual. It has no sales copy.

Brochure Type/Task	1. Grab Attention	2. Make Aware	3. Create Interest	4. Create Enquiry	5. Respond to Enquiry	6. Provide Information	7. Close Sale
Sales	XXXXXXXXXXXXXXXXXXXXXXXXXXXXXXXXXXXXXXXXXX						
Information					XXXXXXXXXXXXXXXXXXXXXXXXXX		
Corporate						XXXXXXXXXXXXX	

3. Checklist and self-assessment for a sales brochure and an information/corporate brochure:

Checklist 3.1: *Winning Sales and Information Brochures*

Sales Brochure	Information/Corporate Brochure
Attention Grabbing? *(9 Marks)* *Does it have stopping power? Will it attract the recipient's interest?*	**Retention?** *(4 Mark)* *Is it attractive and useful enough for client to keep it? Does not need to be attention grabbing.*
Corporate Benefit? *(8 Marks)* *What image does this brochure send to the recipient?* *Cheap brochure = cheap company?* *Dull brochure = dull company?*	**Corporate Benefit?** *(8 Marks)* *Same assessment.*

Legibility? *(8 Marks)*
Does the combination of typeface, point size, leading, measure and layout make copy easy and inviting to read?

Legibility? *(8 Marks)*
Same assessment.

Response? *(7 Marks)*
Is the recipient aware of what will happen next? Have we planned the next step?

Action? *(7 Marks)*
Same assessment.

Instant Message? *(5 Marks)*
Does it communicate a clear, short compelling message?

Presentation? *(5 Marks)*
Quality appearance. Too many pages reduce likelihood of it being read.

Single–Selling Proposition? *(4 Marks)*
Is there one single promise or benefit promoted or a jumble of messages?

Specific Benefits? *(4 Marks)*
Does it communicate all benefits?

Credibility? *(3 Marks)*
Is there hard evidence to support claims? A case history? Third party endorsement?

Credibility? *(5 Marks)*
More important criteria for this type of brochure.

Writing Style? *(2 Marks)*
Has it short words and sentences? Does it use familiar words and images? Is it persuasive?

Writing Style? *(5 Marks)*
Is it informative? Factual? More important criteria for this type of brochure.

Progression? *(2 Marks)*
Is there a logical series of copy that adds up to support the single-selling proposition? Is it easy to understand?

Progression? *(4 Marks)*
More important criteria for this type of brochure.

Impact? *(2 Marks)*
Is the message memorable? Will it be retained for subsequent action?

Impact? *(2 Marks)*
Same assessment.

Award a rating against each criterion, up to the maximum shown in brackets. Add up the score and double it.

Evaluate as follows: 0–60% = not effective; 60%+ score = effective

---

Source: The Marketing Communications Audit – A Company Self-Assessment, Cambridge Strategy Publications, www.cambridgestrategy.com

Exhibitions/Trade Shows/Conferences

Tradeshows and exhibitions are very effective in terms of early stage brand build, introducing new products and generating sales leads for most companies. Research by Deloitte Consulting shows company ranking of the importance and impact of the three main marketing and sales communication tools (see Figure 3.9).

Figure 3.9: *Ranking of Communication Tools by Objective*

Objective	Exhibition	Advertising	Direct Mail
General sales leads	1	2	3
Introduce new products	1	3	2
Taking orders	1	2	3
Promote brand/image	2	1	3
Company awareness	1	2	3
Generate new market	1	2	3

Source: Deloitte & Touche Consulting Group

Checklist 3.2: *Winning Trade Shows and Exhibitions*

Checklist for maximising the use of tradeshows and exhibitions:

1. Do the research to identify/select the best shows for business development.
2. Book a booth in a busy aisle near a big corporate exhibitor that will attract lots of traffic.
3. Be creative about the booth display – the brand is on display and it is impossible to make a first impression the next time a prospect sees it.
4. Time major announcements for the show and create a press-pack. Ask the show's (press) liaison staff to arrange its delivery to the right press reporters and to arrange meetings. Try to set up advance interviews with local radio and press reporters.
5. Schedule the day so that you do not spend all of your time in the booth. Walk the floor to meet/network with:
   * existing customers who are also exhibiting
   * prospective customers
   * possible suppliers
   * "sphere contacts" – other complementary companies to your own that could add value to your product and/or refer prospective customers to you, in return for you doing the same.
6. Develop an appropriate, interesting and distinctive giveaway.

7. Consider scheduling entertainment or an interactive event at the booth or in the evening after the show and issue invitations to customers, prospects, suppliers, contact sphere to attend.
8. Have fruit/bottled water/chocolates on booth tables.
9. Have the most gregarious staff man the booth – well-groomed, attentive, not sitting/talking to one another. Make sure they try to qualify prospects by reference to whether they have buying authority or a product category need, what their purchase timing is and what quantity they would buy.
10. Attend the seminars and stay at the host hotel to network.
11. Develop a "memory hook" to use when you are giving out business cards. For example, "the (Star)-Tech guy from Ireland". This method will help people remember you.
12. When collecting business cards, write a person-specific note on the back of those cards for the more serious prospects for later prioritisation and an angle in following up. Have a well-developed lead-generation and follow-up strategy and system in place.
13. Do not make on-site collateral brochures big and bulky – visitors do not want to carry heavy, awkward material all day. Develop a pocket-friendly brochure or "little book".
14. Bring three times as many business cards as you think you will need.
15. Ask for two cards from serious prospects/contacts – one for you and one for you to give on to your contact sphere. Remember "givers gain"; you help them first and they will reply in kind.

Checklist 3.3: *Winning Conferences*

---

1. **Before the conference:**

• *Test hot topic*	Sample target delegates for their information/advice need – *what would they like to hear/learn?*
• *Check sites*	Check competitor and other conference sites for perspectives on the topic; set up web link to your company.
• *Internal briefing*	Brief all attending staff, client invites.
• *Advertising*	Company credentials/message on adverts/stand/web.
• *Attendance lists*	Mail the attendance list with a conference/post-conference offer – target in particular "pursuit"/"key account" lists.
• *Invitations*	For pursuits, key accounts and staff.
• *Brochure*	Company credentials/message, speaker biog., speech taster.

- *Conference papers*   Speaker's paper printed on company promotional cover.
- *Press/PR*   Issue speaker's paper/covering hot message to press and photo opportunity.

2. **During the conference:**
- *On-site*   Company exhibition unit, brochures, promo, posters, e-disc.
- *Q&A*   Generate question(s) from floor for our speaker's message.
- *Staff percolate*   Company staff to circulate/identify the hot topics. What info needs were met? Which ones were not?
- *Staff targets*   Company staff to meet key account targets and identify/connect with key potential network partners.
- *Make offer*   Reinforce our pre-conference offer.
- *Appointments*   Make the conference offer contingent on an appointment.

3. **After the conference:**
- *Hot topic*   Do the knowledge piece/briefer on the hot topic.
- *Attendance list*   Mail the hot topic briefer to the list.
- *Offer list*   Phone the "offer list" to move to appointment.
- *Appointments*   Confirm and invite.
- *Network/connections*   Agree networker and connections to be followed up. Invite to a post-conference lunch and set up.
- *Article*   Turn speaker paper/hot topic into an article for magazine, newsletter.
- *Database*   Add lists to database.

Open Days

Building trust in your company and its product amongst prospective customers, often in other countries, is one of the biggest marketing challenges that an early stage entrepreneur will face. Having "reference clients" and testimonials is very important, but there is significant brand benefit in having a key prospective customer or group of customers visit your company premises, meet your key management staff and advisors/suppliers. If the benefits to be gained are substantial, the planning, preparation and execution are vital.

Checklist 3.4: *Winning Open Days*

1. **Team selection and briefing.** Decide on the complete group of people in your company that will be "exposed" to the visiting prospects. Remember that first impressions cannot be made a second time. Reception staff/security, executives directly involved in your presentations, executives/staff that will be met on walk-about, etc. should be briefed thoroughly on the impression and messages that need to be conveyed.

2. **Open day nuts and bolts.** The who, what, where and when of the day – attendee details, agenda of presentation/discussions, times, locations, equipment to be used, hospitality arrangements, corporate gifts and transport arrangements.

3. **Objectives.** Define the key objectives you have for the open day. What is the prospective customer expecting from the day? Everyone on the team has to be clear on these factors and on their role/contribution to both.

4. **Strategy.** How will these sets of objectives be achieved? What are the key messages and who will deliver them? Content for the audio/visual/multimedia presentation?

5. **Tactics.** What do we do *if* they ask this or query that? Who handles these questions and how?

6. **Debriefing.** Team meeting to review notes on how the open-day went for both parties. Who might be sponsoring executives in the prospective customer companies? Who might not? Did we influence the decision makers? What worked well? What did not?

Case Studies

Short case studies can be very effective marketing communication tools to build prospective buyer trust in your company and its products. For best effect, case studies should:

- Be short, no more than 300–500 words, and specific
- Have a consistent format/structure – best done with three headings:

  1. The challenge or burning issue addressed
  2. The solution/approach to resolve
  3. The results/situation now achieved

- Be real and credible, with a "pain-point" and quantification
- Be easily accessible and understood.

Testimonials

As a new business, to make the sale of a new product in a new market, the prospective customer's natural scepticism must be overcome and a relationship of trust built. When others (satisfied customers, commentators and experts) say good things about you and your product, it lessens the scepticism and distrust. It is the critical part of the positioning statement – it can be the proof statement on the USP.

Testimonials are powerfully persuasive and they keep on working. In order to obtain a testimonial that becomes part of the positioning statement, you should:

- Try to get a testimonial from a recognised/influential commentator or expert on how well the product addresses and solves a problem for consumers in the target audience
- Try to get the product assessed and graded or commented on in awards programmes
- Try to get a customer testimonial as soon as possible after the customer buys – preferably within a week
- Only target customers who will have credibility and will be a reference for your market position. They should be an ideal representation of the target customer group
- Always ask them to include the following in their testimonial:

  - the USP of the product
  - the difficulty they had experienced before buying your product
  - their credentials
  - a photograph of them with your product.

Always get their permission to use their testimonial in your marketing communications and if they are slow in writing it for you, offer a draft for them to edit.

Once testimonial(s) have been generated and collected, use them in the marketing communications programme.

1. Post them on the website, on different pages and in borders so they remain in view
2. Create a simple A4 Word document entitled "What People Say ...", containing the testimonials; leave it in reception and on tables at the exhibition booth and include it in all press-publicity packs
3. Include a testimonial in advertisements
4. In direct marketing/mailings, include a separate sheet/version of "What People Say ..."
5. Leverage the relationship with customers who have provided you with good testimonials into lots more of their type. Run a *referral programme* or *drive* every year – surprise them when they least

expect it by, for example, sending them a lottery ticket for a big jackpot or offering a prize/cash bonus to the customer who gave the most warm referrals in a given period.

Publicity

Publicity or public relations is about communicating in a planned and strategic way with key "publics" that potentially have an interest in you, the company, the products and so on and in whom you have a vested interest in terms of, for example:

- Promoting/reinforcing the brand/product positioning
- Introducing new products
- Announcing significant developments, personnel changes/additions, achievements, awards, strategic partnerships, alliances, new offices, geographical expansion
- Offering your expertise/commentary on a specific business arena, industry or marketplace
- Defending/explaining a business-threatening issue.

Publicity is a very powerful and underused marketing tool and can contribute significantly to brand building at a lower cost than advertising. It comprises typically three distinct sets of communication activities: media/press relations, public affairs and crisis management. It is a distinctive and valuable marketing communications tool, in so far that as a mass-market tool:

- It is not as expensive as advertising in print, broadcast and outdoor media.
- It has legs. Publicity such as an article/feature in a magazine can be remembered far longer than an advertisement. As a component of an integrated marketing communications programme, it provides a continuous background effect of making the other communication tool messages credible.
- It has "perceived credibility". Audiences perceive a magazine article or newspaper feature has more credibility than a "paid-for" advertisement.

For the start up and emerging stage entrepreneur, the most immediate usage of publicity and its component communication tools will be the following three. Again, as in other marketing communications, the brand/product positioning statement drives the PR strategy and the messages to be delivered.

1.   Press Release/Interviews

Be Specific – Who?

First and last in terms of importance is "Know your customer". Who are the reporters/journalists that you want to target for an ongoing relationship of mutually meeting one another's needs and in what publications and media?

Be Specific – What?

Press releases: should be written in a direct, straightforward style. Short and terse is great. The ideal length is one to three pages. Use a font that is easy to read (Times New Roman, Arial or Helvetica). Have a one and a half spacing.

At the top of the page is the *attention-grabber* headline. This will be informative (not sensational) and will be the essence of the news/message. Next comes the important *lead-off* paragraph, which is the first paragraph of the body of the release. This starts with a dateline (actual date of official release) and city/country. It covers the journalist's interest in the who, what, when, where, how and why. Next, you *make your case* by bolstering/expanding on the points made in the lead paragraph. This can include a full description of a new product, quotes from executives on a new product's features and an insightful endorsement from a customer. Finally, you *end* and give "further information" contact details.

Journalist interviews: the objective is *not* to simply answer questions. You have three or four particular positioning-statement points you want to get across. Firstly, *know your story*. What is the headline you want to see and what are the three themes that you want to see in the body text? Your story should make your audience respond favourably to you. Your goal is therefore to communicate those themes early and often, using a few simple sentences. If it is a new product, explain why the marketplace needs a new solution (the problem), describe the new product and how it works (the USP) and use facts/figures and anecdotes to provide a sense of successful launch or purchase into the market. Control the interview: it is important that you guide the journalist to what is important and tell your story *your way*. Journalists know they will usually get an interesting response by playing devil's advocate in their questioning – do not repeat negative language/questions and do not dwell on the matter.

2.   Public Affairs

There are two main publics to be targeted here. The first is the *business influencers audience*, for example trade associations, chambers of commerce and so on. The second is the *government/regulatory audiences*. Both groups are important sources of information about political, regulatory and legal developments and about trends that may impact upon your business. They are publics that become important audiences for influencing, to minimise or eradicate prospective negative legal/regulatory issues.

In addition to regulatory/legal matters, the business influencers audience is a natural group for networking and developing contact spheres.

3.   Crisis Management

Although unlikely, it is still possible that something could go wrong – say, your product has unforeseen implications or impacts for buyers – and you could need to manage various relevant and potentially relevant audiences. Most obvious is the media, but others externally may include existing clients, investors and regulators; others internally may include your staff, suppliers, partners and distributors. Here are the positive and negative actions in handling a crisis:

Checklist 3.5: *Crisis Response*

Positive Actions	Negative Actions
Make appropriate and caring response to the public – showing concern for those affected.	Being unprepared. "No Comment" is not an option.
Use a few carefully worded messages – communicating that the problem has been identified and that steps are being taken to solve it.	Issuing "company defensive centric" responses.
Be open and available to the media.	Trying to downplay or downsize the problem.
Comment early to define the issue and scope/shape the debate.	Trying to blame others.
Provide factual information quickly – reduce opportunities for speculation and misinformation.	Waiting for more evidence or information before acting.
Communicate all bad news at once.	Going it solo – use an external advisor.
Keep all stakeholders informed.	Focusing on technical/legal aspects to the exclusion of public relations.
Use the crisis as an opportunity to educate and increase awareness of good things about the company.	Misclassifying the crisis.
Have a crisis-handling plan and team.	Fighting legislative/regulatory activity when it clearly expresses the will of the public.
Do regular "risk" audits.	
Be prepared to bear short-term cost to preserve trust through a crisis.	

Selecting your Media Relations Agency

Careful consideration should be given to the selection of the right media relations agency. Media relations is very important in building a venture's brand.

Template 6: *Request for Proposal for Media Relations Services to Company X*

Request for Proposal Content/Sections

Introduction
Background to the company, its key executives and drivers for requirement.

Proposal Outline
You are invited to tender for this work through the submission of a detailed proposal to include:
- agency credentials (including client list, team credentials and date of incorporation)
- outline of service development and delivery capability on offer
  - planning techniques
  - implementation processes
  - resources for growing media opportunities
  - performance metrics
  - client case studies
  - creative treatment capability and relevant examples
  - client references
- outline view of ideal contents of a media relations plan.

Reporting Lines
The successful agency will be responsible for delivering against a detailed co-developed media relations plan, managed on a day-to-day basis by marketing manager, PR, and the in-house media-relations team.

Scope of Company XXX's Requirements

- The firm's requirements are best illustrated at this stage by the following documents (attached), which you are asked not to copy, distribute or share with any parties outside the agency ...

Terms and Conditions
If successful, you will be required to sign a service level agreement similar to the one attached which in effect becomes an operational contract, notwithstanding your own terms and conditions. The contract would include:
- specified performance metrics (output/activity and outcome)
- agreed notional retainer fee (paid monthly in arrears to include expenses)
- agreed service level performance reward (to supplement monthly fees, paid each quarter)
- one month notice period.

The Tendering Process

If you wish to accept our invitation to tender you will be required, within the next two weeks, to take the following steps:

- submit, in writing, a tender document as outlined in this paper to be delivered to the marketing manager, PR
- if successful at above step, present your proposal to the marketing director and manager.

If you are then short-listed (no more than three agencies), you will be requested to hone aspects of the proposal and prepare a PR creative/execution direction for one of the four programmes/profiles attaching for a final presentation to the managing director and marketing director and manager, PR. It is our intention to appoint an agency by ...

Checklist 3.6: *Media Relations Agency Proposal Performance Appraisal*

1. Did the agency submit a good brochure/video/proposal?

2. Did the agency submit this promptly?

3. Does the agency meet our criteria, in terms of
   - location
   - size/turnover of staff
   - average size of client
   - length in existence
   - financial stability
   - quality of client list
   - experience in similar markets
   - provision of required services
   - quality of work
   - results obtained for clients
   - international coverage?

4. Does the character and tone of the agency fit our needs?

5. Is the agency's creative work
   - distinctive
   - professional and single-minded
   - well executed
   - achieving obvious client results?

6. Is there anything special/distinctive/different about the agency?

7. Did the agency try to fit its reply to our needs?

8. Does the agency offer the latest resources for growing media opportunities?

9. Fee proposal: retainer
                            bonus

10. Query/issues

11. Ranking

Direct Marketing

Direct marketing is about direct communication with individual customers or prospects to obtain an immediate response or cultivate a lasting relationship. Beyond brand and image building, direct marketing seeks direct, immediate and measurable responses. The principal forms of direct marketing include direct-mail marketing, online marketing, SMS text, telemarketing, catalogue marketing, kiosk marketing and direct-response TV. Personal selling on a face2face basis also involves direct marketing.

Direct-mail marketing: sending an offer, announcement, reminder or other item (for example a "dimensional marketing piece" such as an executive toy) to a person at a particular address. It is a commonly used marketing communications tool, with obvious cost-effectiveness benefits.

Online marketing: often used as a response mechanism option for the prospective customer to learn more about, for example, a press-advertised offer or used as an e-mail offer with a link back to a dedicated website/micro-site within your main website for more details on the offer. Can also be used to survey prospective and existing clients as part of ongoing market intelligence gathering or about a new product.

SMS text: using mobile phone texting to make an offer and solicit response call to a telemarketing centre or run competitions to identify segments for subsequent offer making.

Telemarketing: using dedicated phone/staff to generate and qualify prospective leads for a sale, respond to and qualify prospective leads generated by advertising or direct marketing tools (direct mail or online), sell to prospects and customers, service customers' accounts and survey/gather market intelligence. Key qualifying questions by telemarketing staff are: Has the prospect buying authority? Have they the product need? Is the purchase timing right? What might be the purchase quantities/value?

Catalogue marketing: print or electronic catalogues that are sent to select customer bases or made available in stores.

Kiosk marketing: information and ordering machines/facilities in areas where target prospects frequently gather in large numbers.

Direct-response TV/Channels: dedicated TV and channels for purchase by customers, usually involving a call-centre response mechanism. Suitable for low-involvement/low-risk purchases and often impulse buys.

In direct-mail marketing the following are essential to a cost-effective outcome:

1. Direct mailers cite the 60–30–10 rule. That means success depends 60% on the quality and accuracy of your "list", 30% on your "offer" and 10% on "creativity".
2. The most powerful words to use in direct mail include:
   you/your new today because enjoy announcing limited free now since off at last only then
3. Typical direct mail offers include (free, no obligation, nominal priced):
   information trial book catalogue survey demo consultation sample gift

---

Checklist 3.7: *All Direct Marketing Communications*

---

1. Copy text has to be accessible to the would-be reader. Present everything in bite-size chunks or paragraphs of no more than three lines long. Present key selling proposition(s) as bullet point(s). Use bold and underline to draw attention to key ideas.
2. Page or screen should be at least 45 per cent white space.
3. Present call-to-action early and often. No later than the third paragraph.
4. In nearly every sentence, express a benefit and write the benefit first.
5. Sell the offer, not the product. Concentrate on selling the benefits of responding and receiving the offer. If it is ultimately a high-involvement/high-risk purchase, then concentrate on selling the benefits of the "giver first" offer.
6. Use the customer "you" language, do not talk about "our" company and "our" products. Keep it action orientated and use active language.
7. Finally, run your eye over the headlines, subheadings, indents, underlined phrases and see if they talk your offer convincingly as follows:

   - pain or opportunity gain identified
   - benefit offer made

- call to action
- benefit and offer description
- call to action
- reason to respond now
- benefit summary
- call to action.

Template 7: *Direct Mail Marketing*

DIRECT/DIMENSIONAL MAILING PROCESS

Mailing Campaign Specification for:

1.   Mailing Campaign Objectives

_____

_____

_____

_____

_____

_____

_____

Indirect effect on sales ←						→ Direct effect on sales
☐	☐	☐	☐	☐	☐	
1. Reinforce attitudes (reinforce existing behaviours)	2. Modify attitudes (change future existing behaviours)	3. Recall satisfaction (reinforce needs behaviours)	4. Relate brand to own	5. Seek info	6. Buy	

2.   Audience Being Targeted: ☐ **Active involved consumers**

☐ **Inactive, uninvolved potential future consumers**

_____

_____

_____

_____

_____

_____

| Low involvement in product category/ low interest in direct message ← | | | | → High involvement in product category/ high interest in direct message |

| ☐ | ☐ | ☐ | ☐ | ☐ |

| 1. No perceived need for product category | 2. Recognition of latent product need | 3. Passive consideration of product need | 4. Search/review of product choices | 5. Purchase product |

Communication Message(s)	Awareness	Interest	Information/advice	Evaluation	Action

3. The Mailing Proposition:

_____
_____
_____
_____
_____

4. The Proposition Delivery Package:

_____   ☐ Letter
_____   ☐ Outer envelope
_____   ☐ Brochure/dimensional package
_____   ☐ Response/follow-up mechanisms
_____   ☐ Teaser/offer
_____
_____
_____
_____
_____
_____

5. Why is the Proposition/Package Right?

Right Prospect?   Describe the prospect we want to "talk to", their motivations, their key need, greed and level of interest and understanding.

_____
_____
_____
_____

Right Message?   Describe how the proposition meets the prospect's key needs.

_____
_____
_____
_____

Right Time?   Is there a "responsive time" when need/greed motivations are high(est)? Is time required to enable communication, build trust and enable reception of the message?

_____
_____
_____
_____

Right Way?   How does the delivery package create the right mental picture/subliminal image of us/our proposition? Will it create opportunity for follow-up and future mailings to be well received? Does it create urge to respond? Within a time-frame?

_____
_____
_____
_____

6. What Are the Campaign Implementation Processes and who Is Responsible?

_____   ☐ Proposition preparation
_____   ☐ Proposition delivery package
_____   ☐ Mailing
_____   ☐ Inbound response
_____   ☐ Fulfilment
_____   ☐ Outbound follow-up
_____   ☐ Appointment
_____   ☐ Feedback
_____   ☐ Repeat mailing(s)
_____   ☐ Analysis

_____
_____
_____
_____
_____
_____
_____
_____

7.   What Is the Budget?

☐ List purchase/cleansing
☐ Proposition delivery package
☐ Mailing(s)
☐ Inbound/outbound handling
☐ Analysis

Direct E-Mail Marketing

There are many reasons why e-mail marketing activity is being used increasingly as a powerful communication tool in acquiring, retaining and servicing customers.

- E-mail is the number-one reason why people turn on their computer.
- Half of consumers say they would be more likely to purchase online from an opt-in e-mail campaign.
- Nearly two-thirds of consumers subscribe to one or more e-mail newsletters.
- B2B e-mail newsletters have a 20 per cent higher open rate than B2B direct e-mail.
- Opt-in e-mail produces an average response rate of 4–15 per cent.
- Two-thirds of companies surveyed in the US by the Direct Marketing Association said their sales in 2001 increased as a result of using e-mail marketing. Medium-sized companies reported the best results, with 59.8 per cent seeing an increase from last year. Large companies reported a 47.1 per cent increase and small companies said their sales rose 42.6 per cent because of e-mail promotions.
- In 2002, more US businesses were using e-mail marketing campaigns, instead of traditional direct postal mailings.
- While 13 per cent of respondents said they allocated *their total marketing budget* to e-mail marketing, smaller companies generally allocated the highest percentage, 21.4 per cent. Large companies allocated 13.4 per cent and medium-sized companies allocated 7 per cent of their total marketing budgets. Nearly two-thirds of respondents said they were able to manage their e-mail marketing in-house.

E-Mail Marketing Best Practices

Putting the right offer in front of the right person at the right time can produce tremendous results for new customer acquisition, customer loyalty and customer retention. In order to deploy the most effective campaigns and realise the highest response rates, you must do a certain amount of planning and consider a number of proven, results-oriented e-marketing techniques. *Never spam or indiscriminately issue e-mails.*

Message

Keep it brief – one or two short paragraphs whose sole aim is to trigger a response/next step. Incentives can increase response to a call-to-action. It is also better to use the following fonts for your e-mail:

- Courier New
- Lucida Console
- Letter Gothic

Stay within standard line lengths – about 76 characters. If you go wider than this, not all e-mail clients will be able to clearly read your message. To preserve your formatting, insert hard returns at 60/65 characters per line of text in your e-mail.

Segment Lists

Chop your database into smaller, segmented slices based on client or target preferences and past behaviour. Careful segmentation will help you focus your efforts and make your campaigns more relevant to the consumer.

Targeted Offers

Prospects and customers will be more likely to respond to messages that match their interest set. Use historical data to apply what you know about the likes and dislikes of your target market segments. Keep the subject line brief and compelling. Create specific messages for specific audiences. Do not over-do e-mailing to your lists. Establish and stick to a frequency: monthly newsletter, bi-weekly offers and urgent updates as needed.

Tailored to Fit

Personalising e-mail content will help to retain the consumer's interest and will add relevance. In the world of direct e-marketing, everyone is unique and one size does not fit all. Always identify yourself as the sender – otherwise the risk of binning increases.

Quality over Quantity

Boost response rates by creating offers for unique products, useful information, compelling content, special pricing or gifts. Again, match the offer to the segment. Every message in a customer's inbox requires time and attention. If you do not deliver valuable offers, your customers will opt out of your mailing list.

Call-to-Action

Your campaign's primary objective should be to have prospects take action. Examples include "Click to ... link to more information/ buy/join/communicate with a sales representative/participate in a survey/play in a contest/refer a friend". Incentives can increase response to a call-to-action.

Sales versus Marketing

Many marketers think the web is primarily a direct sales medium, rather than a multifaceted communications tool that can be used to create sales activities in other channels. Decide which sales channel your campaign is going to support.

Text versus HTML

Give your customers the option of receiving messages in text or HTML format. Some people prefer text to graphics. Give it to them their way. HTML e-mail generates much higher response rates than text (but some e-mail browsers cannot view it).

Micro-Sites/Landing Site

Giving respondents a micro-website to respond to rather than just an e-mail address creates more interaction and measurement opportunities. Plus, a picture paints a thousand words. The quality and functionality of your landing pages have the most impact on conversion rates

Online/Offline Integration

Create a micro-website as a response option for your offline (direct mail, display ads) promotions. Again, you will create opportunities to interact with your customers.

No Spam

Do not send unsolicited e-mails. Spam messages are unwelcome. You will damage your company's reputation by sending unwanted e-mails.

Respect the Customer

Messages and offers that go to unresponsive consumers week after week are no better than spam. Make it easy for people to unsubscribe, access and change data.

Measure and Report

Tracking the actions of your customers and prospects is critical to your success. After deploying several campaigns, you will have generated a mountain of response information. Analyse it and use it when creating new offers and new approaches. And remember that technology is a magical tool for marketing wizards to use – but it does not replace the wizard.

Your Website

Knowing the key words that your prospective customers use in searching for suppliers in your category is crucial in making your website highly visible in your target marketplace. Ask target clients for their "search words" and/or look at the *keyword suggestion tool* (http://inventory. overture.com/d/searchinventory/suggestion/). When you know these key words, make sure you put them into the title tag, the description meta-tag, the keywords meta-tag and, in the first few paragraphs of your homepage, body copy. In addition to using the keywords employed in your marketplace, you should also get listed in the top search engines: Google.com, Alltheweb.com, Yahoo.com, Search.msn.com, Lycos.com, Askjeeves.com and Looksmart.com.

Personal Selling

The original, oldest form of direct marketing is the sales call/pitch. In start up to emerging stage businesses, the entrepreneur leads the sales function and, in many cases, does not have a background in marketing (generating the prospective buyers) and sales (presenting, negotiating and closing the product buy). Initial sales success can be largely carried as a result of the entrepreneur's deep product and problem knowledge and their passion for what they are building. This will continue to be critically important.

However, as the business grows, a sales infrastructure has to be put in place to give effect to the business's positioning and segmentation. In terms of sales staff, this may include a direct or field sales force, selling directly to the end customer and/or a business development team devoted to forming, sustaining and motivating relationships with third parties who sell the product to the end customer. It may also include outsourcing sales to a third party representative who carries a number of manufacturers' products into the market segment you want to reach.

When the positioning statement for attracting the end customer market and the positioning statement for attracting the intermediary network are established and defined, common to both are the following:

1. Defining the sales process steps and techniques to be used in moving the customer from prospect to purchaser. The steps and techniques must be fully consistent with the business positioning and brand.
2. Recruiting sales staff to operate the sales process and sales managers (business development managers) to manage, motivate and deliver the selling action.
3. Providing the key sales-process tools for sales/business development staff to use.
4. Remuneration and performance management.

Sales Process

This is the foundation for success.

- *The best sales process is the customer's desired buying process.*
- *Without a well-developed and defined sales process, the business is vulnerable to random excellence and disaster in equal measure.*

The defined sales process ensures consistency and efficiency in delivery of the positioning to the defined target audience through all sales channels. Much of the detail of the best sales process will come from:

1. How well you understand the type of company/industry (or consumer type) and their key drivers for success
2. The answers your customers gave when asked in research about how they ideally would like to buy from their (described) ideal supplier and
3. How your business team then takes each step and element and defines a brand-position-consistent way of delivering the sales process.

Figure 3.10: *A Willing Buy Is a Successful Sale*

Nothing is Ever Sold Successfully until the Customer Willingly Buys

A customer buying process will evolve through the following sequential steps:

- I am important and want to be respected.
- You must consider my needs.
- You must first earn my trust.
- How will your solutions help me (the benefits)?
- What are the facts?
- What are the snags?
- What do I have to do?
- I agree/disagree.

Structuring the Sales Force

Once you have segmented your target market, identified the target audience's buying process and devised your positioning, you will find that the best way to structure, equip and manage your sales force will be apparent.

Figure 3.11: *Structuring the Sales Force*

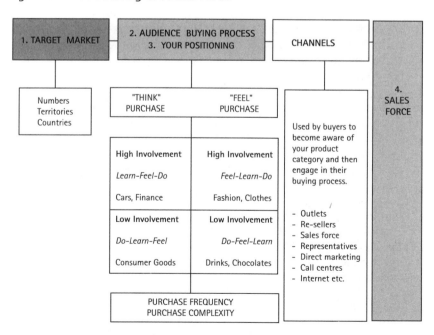

Let us assume that the product being positioned to a corporate buyer is a high-involvement complex sale. It demands the active involvement of a buyer/group to ensure that the perceived high-risk of an adverse outcome is minimised. It probably represents a buy of over $150,000 and will be decided by a buying committee of upwards of twelve people.

The key to sales success in this sales process is in the positioning of the sales person and the required "give first" to earn the buyer executive's trust and respect. Unfortunately, however, it is a fact that C-Suite executive buyers will not perceive a sales person as their peer. This happens in consumer markets too. Look at the financial services market (perceived complex purchase) where financial companies have to position their sales staff as personal financial advisors and where they in turn must offer a give first (usually a guide to some aspect of finance) to gain the buyer's trust.

In complex business purchases, buyers will give their trust only to a business peer who provides them with a give first of valuable insight, information and resource that measurably contributes value to their current situation (i.e. their marketplace, industry, challenges, risks and competition, and financial position) and to their future state (where they want to get to). Structuring a sales force in this example is primarily about the appropriate type of seller needed – i.e. a small team of consultative sales professionals (drawn possibly from an advisory position to or in the targeted industry).

Sales Staff Recruitment and Management

Recruiting the right sales staff and management and then organising how they are best structured will be a lot less fraught with failure if there is clarity about the above. There are risks to hiring a competitor's sales staff, for example they may bring bad industry habits with them. Many see the benefits of hiring outside the industry, but in a relevant "involvement level" sale area, and training the new employees to get best fit with the company's brand and values. Candidates that have held at least two prior jobs in different companies, providing that one of those was in sales, are more likely to be focused on choosing your company for its culture and as a career.

Good salespeople use four building blocks to establish customer trust:

1. **Competence:** deep knowledge of the problem area and product solution inspires customer confidence
2. **Reliability:** being able to rely on the sales person to do what they say they will do, when promised
3. **Intentions:** it is natural to trust those whose intentions are to help
4. **Appearance:** clean car, well-groomed, professional appearance, good posture, broad vocabulary, clear voice and frequent eye contact.

Good sales managers commit themselves 100 per cent to the success of their sales staff and teach by example, using instruction and positive feedback. They meet with each salesperson at least once a month to identify any problems and prescribe 30-day programmes to reach next-level performance. The sales manager must exhibit high performance standards: they "do-it-now" with decisions, they do not become buddies, they do not spend time with poor performers, they are "problem-attackers" and they allow risk-taking. Good managers praise in public and reprimand in private.

Sales Remuneration and Management

Realistic goals are key and should be based on a sound understanding of the product category/industry 100–50–10–5 dynamic, i.e. it takes a pool of 100 prospects to extract 50 contacts to get in front of 10 interested customers and secure 5 sales closes. Open-ended earning potential really turns sales staff on. Ongoing motivational incentives keep the activity levels up.

Earnings for a salesperson involved in the consultative, complex selling process in the US are typically about $120,000; for relationship selling, they average $90,000; and for transactional, less complex selling, they average $60,000. How much of that is "fixed/basic" and how much is "performance" depends on whether team players are being sought and on the set of actions/goals the company wants to achieve (margin, new product take up, etc.). If a salesperson has to exercise a large amount of influence to get the sales, then a large proportion of earnings should be "performance". Low-value and re-buy sales lend themselves to commission only, while big-value and one-off buys lend themselves to fixed pay.

Examples of monetary incentives for sales staff are a 10 per cent monthly pay bonus if sales are up 20 per cent on last year's, a 20 per cent monthly pay bonus if sales are up 40 per cent on last year's, plus an extra month's pay if the firm's financial targets are met. Examples of non-monetary incentives include time off, article in company newsletter, trophy at special recognition event, lottery tickets or tickets to concerts.

Sales Manner and Face2Face Technique

Sales manner is about balancing *projection* and *empathy*. Projection is about how the sales person comes across to the customer – their style, personality, authority, expertise and confidence. Empathy is about being perceived by the customer as seeing things from their perspective, i.e. putting yourself in the customer's shoes.

There are five critical success factors in any sales meeting:

1. You must set and drive the agenda
2. Open up and analyse the customer's needs with questions on background/current state, problems and their implications, perceived needs and priority actions
3. Present solutions to those priority needs in the following four ways: make the solutions understandable, make them attractive, make them convincing and secure feedback that these have been achieved
4. Deal with resistance
5. Obtain a willing commitment to proceed further.

In dealing with customers, it can be helpful to adjust your sales emphasis to their personality type.

Figure 3.12: *Buyer Personality Types*

TASK Personality the problem solved, process, steps	DETAILS Personality the costs saved, specifications
IDEA Personality the opportunities opened up, big picture	PEOPLE Personality testimonials, references

Sales Tools

The key sales tools required by the sales staff to deliver the sales process are the well-researched and understood desired buying process of the buyer, sales guides and sales materials. A good sales guide educates the sales force on who the target audience is, about the product's unique features and benefits (in relation to the buyer's desired buying needs and process, and as compared to the key competitors and their offerings/positioning), the "proof", or why the target customer should believe you, and finally the testimonials. This guide forms a key training tool and ensures consistent delivery of the business positioning.

Sales materials that need to be created for use at the right stages of the buying (flip for sales) process – Awareness/Interest/Desire/Action – are corporate brochures, sales brochures, information brochures and pitch presentations. The brochures and their use are described in the "Corporate/Product Brochures" section on page 55.

Presentations will typically have two key communication tools: the first is the entrepreneur and a second team member as communicators; the second is a PowerPoint presentation and presentation folder. At pitch meetings, it is clearly important to get it right and make the favourable first impression. This cannot be done alone; it is impossible to pitch, present and listen at the same time. Here are some guidelines on delivering a PowerPoint presentation:

1. Do not make the mistake of many and deliver an "All About Us" presentation, which goes like this: who we are, our history, our clients, our team, our credentials, why we are different, our fees, etc. There is nothing in this type of presentation for the customer, their problems, their issues and their concerns, and the solutions you can really offer them.

2. Do not use templates, particularly where you then have to cram the slide with information. At least 45 per cent of the slide should be white space. Graphics should be used, to the point of replacing text. Studies show that, in a presentation, a combination of the spoken word and graphics is the best and most engaging formula for audience involvement and understanding. Do not use your logo on every page.

3. Relax a little at the start and create a personal connection – the audience will be trying to figure out if you are the kind of person they can work with and trust. People buy people first. Use an anecdote.

4. Your audience is at their most attentive during the opening and closing stages of your presentation, so make sure you get your messages across at these critical stages. Use pauses and silences to punctuate your presentation and draw in your audience. After delivering a key point, accentuate it by stopping, standing still and moving only your eyes around the table. Energy levels are also important – vary your levels to keep the audience alert and engaged.

5. Listen, Listen, Listen. Most people think they do, but in reality they are thinking ahead to the next point they are going to make in their presentation and therefore miss key buying/selling signals and queries. Very often, it is your performance in terms of listening and responding on your feet at the presentation that dictate a successful outcome.

6. Do not assume the audience has read any of the documentation that you sent in advance.

7. Do not give a hand-out before your presentation – it can distract attention away from your presentation, as people flick through pages.

8. Prepare answers to questions in advance and know how to handle questions that you will not answer at the presentation. Some things should not be discussed at an initial or large group meeting, such as fees, when the project is not known at that point.

9. Set a follow-up and establish a clear statement of what will happen next – do not expect them to ask for it.

Proposals/Responding to Request for a Proposal

In research on the qualities that business buyers want from their professional services suppliers, three key success factors are sought:

Figure 3.13: *Key Criteria for a Buyer of Professional Services*

CHEMISTRY

At ease discussing issues

Confident you will do the job

Cares about my agenda

TRUST

CUSTOMER

These are relevant for most proposal teams. Prospective customers in a proposal process evaluate you from the moment you pick up the phone to arrange the first meeting up to (and including) the last question answered at the oral presentation. They are looking for chemistry, customer focus and trust in the team that they will be dealing with. There are six winning principles for proposals:

1. Pre-qualify and select the best team. The best team must be able to win and do the work.
2. Plan and manage a campaign to influence the client. A proposal is a competition, not a document. There are many buyers to influence.
3. Manage the team's performance to make a positive impression at all meetings. It is critical to match team members with their "opposite number" on the client side and make sure they connect at the right times and meetings. Use meetings to convince clients they should buy from you. Your questions should show your customer focus and build the chemistry and trust.
4. If you can and where you can, even in the smallest ways, co-develop a specific and interesting approach with the client and use the proposal document to confirm it.
5. Present effectively as a team at orals. It is the last opportunity for the client to differentiate amongst competitors. It is critical to engage the client and impart a final positive impression. They may not remember exact details, but they will remember how you said it.

6. Your proposal document, where you have leverage to free-text it, should have a structure that has a logical framework and is easy for the client to follow, contains your key selling messages that are customer focussed, uses the client's terminology, demonstrates appropriate creativity and uses examples, case studies and testimonials.

Pitches: Elevator, Lobby and Fifteen Minute

In advance of any exhibition, conference or presentation of your company to an external prospective stakeholder audience (supplier, buyer, partner, investor, financier, employee recruitment, etc.), you need to have three versions of your pitch ready.

Version 1: Elevator
This is your very brief 30-second pitch to hook a prospect into finding out more from you and/or mentally positioning you for future reference. For example:

"I work with (*target audience*) who need (*the solution/end benefit*) so that (*the value proposition*) because right now (*the big problem*) ..."

Version 2: Lobby
Your lobby version then extends the elevator pitch by including *reference customers* for whom you have already solved problems, giving examples of the financial and other benefits delivered and amplifying both the big problem and the uniqueness of your value proposition.

Version 3: Fifteen Minutes
Use an A4 desk flip chart to present yourself and your company in just ten key slides.

Figure 3.14: *The 15-Minute Sales Pitch to a Funder*

Ten must-have slides:

1. Cover – business positioning statement
2. Market – the need and what customers have it
3. Solution – product, core benefit, USP
4. Competitive position – who the competing suppliers are
5. Marketing/sales/support – channels/partners and team
6. Business strategy – your business mission and values
7. Financial projections – financial position
8. Funding sought – investors
9. Management – relevant experience
10. Milestones – product development, for example

Sales Promotions

Sales promotions are used to identify and attract new customers, launch new products, motivate the sales force and increase take-up by re-sellers or intermediaries. Here are some of the more frequently used consumer and trade sales promotion techniques:

Consumer
- Coupons
- Demonstrations
- Free samples
- Frequent-user incentive
- Multiple-pack incentive
- Money refunds/guarantees
- Consumer contests, games and gifts

Trade
- Free merchandise
- Co-operative advertising
- Sales contests
- Buying allowance or discount for volume
- Dealer loader or gift for volume purchases

Figure 3.15: *Using Guarantees as a Promotional Tool*

Using guarantees as a sales promotion tool
What makes for a good guarantee?
It should be:

1. Unconditional and cover only elements that you fully control
2. Easy to understand and communicate
3. Meaningful in terms of covering what is important to the customer and meaningful in financial terms
4. Easy to invoke by the customer, no hoops and loops to go through
5. Easy to collect and effect.

Why guarantees work
Guarantees work well in promotions because:

1. They force focus on the customer and what is important to them
2. They set clear standards for employees to follow
3. They generate valuable customer feedback, opportunities to learn about errors/breakdowns

4. They reduce the customer's FUD (fear, uncertainty and doubt) and risk in the buying process.

Guarantees work best
Guarantees work best in the following buyer/market contexts:

1. The purchase price is significant (upfront and/or down the line)
2. The buyer has little experience/expertise in the area
3. The negative outcomes of a product failure/bad buying decision are high and costly in financial/other ways
4. The industry has a less-than-wholesome image with consumers for quality
5. The company offering the guarantee needs frequent customer repurchases
6. The company offering the guarantee will be deeply affected by word of mouth in the marketplace.

Template 8: *Brand/Product Position Statement – To Drive All Marketing Communications – During the Emerging Stage*

Brand Values of the Company	Existing	Desired/New
What are the key values held by customers, staff, suppliers competitors and influencers about the company?		
• existing • desired/new ...		
Key Customer Needs and Values		
Describe the customer's desired or expected needs under each of these four key dimensions of the customer buying experience:		
1. Service experience expectation, the key "moments of truth" when it would be delivered and ranking of moments	**Service Experience and "moments of truth"**	
2. Sales experience expectation from how they would become aware of the product, channels through which they would: become knowledgeable about its benefits to them, have questions dealt with and action a purchase	**Sales Experience**	

3. Product features and benefits that meet and/or exceed their key needs in the product category and that are not delivered by competitors

Products

_____

_____

_____

4. End goal statement of the customer, setting out in a sentence or two what economic social, personal objective they will achieve with the product.

End Goal

_____

_____

_____

Key Message(s)

What are the key brand-positioning messages to be used in all marketing communications?

- brochure/collaterals
- web
- publicity
- exhibitions/events
- direct marketing
- personal selling
- promotions
- sponsorship
- advertising (print, radio, TV, outdoor, cinema, channels, SMS, PDAs)

_____

_____

_____

_____

_____

_____

_____

_____

_____

_____

Key Target Customers

Who are the primary target customers (clients and prospects)? Describe by way of demographic, geographic, industrial, personal, purchase attributes, etc.

Describe them with reference to their segmentation profile and descriptor variables, grouping together segments with similar requirements and buying characteristics.

Primary

_____

_____

_____

Secondary

_____

_____

_____

Product USP	The USPs
The unique benefits offered that • meet the following key customer needs and values • are also different to (or not offered by) the competition • are perhaps sustainable advantages/not easily copied.	_____ _____ _____ _____ _____ _____
Key Interest by Customer Segments Which products or customer needs are specific to the different customer segments?	_____ _____ _____ _____ _____
Differentiation How is the company brand/product different from those of the key competitors?	_____ _____ _____ _____ _____

Template 9: *Corporate Brand – Integrated Marketing Communication Programme for Start Up and Emerging Stage*

- **Marketing objectives:** adoption of new product amongst early adopter/innovator customers/segments. Securing initial early majority customers. Start to build trust in company through brand.
- **Communication strategies:** create awareness and interest among innovators and early adopters.
- **Communication media:** publicity, personal selling, advertising and promotion.

Activity	Role	Key Values/Initiatives	Audience
Brand – corporate • Name • Logo • Identity • Company we keep actions Brand – product adoption	Associate company name/logo with Product category Need Build trust and credibility Build trust and credibility	Position central messages Tag line	Prospects Customers Staff Intermediaries Influencers
Literature • Sales guides • Sales brochures • Sales information • Corporate	Reinforce brand and product positioning	Position central messages Tag line	Prospects Customers Staff Intermediaries Influencers
Advertising TV Press Radio Outdoor Cinema	Promote brand positioning Affect sales by inspiring audience to seek information	Position central messages Tag line	Prospects Customers Staff Intermediaries Influencers
Public relations – consumer	Raise awareness Stimulate interest Reinforce brand positioning Inform/educate	Position central messages Tag line	Prospects Customers Staff Intermediaries Influencers
Public relations – trade	Raise awareness Reinforce brand positioning Educate/inform	Position central messages Tag line	Prospects Customers Staff Intermediaries
Sponsorship	Raise awareness Reinforce (new) prop	Education/product category needs awareness	Prospects Customers Staff Intermediaries
Personal selling Direct sales force • Sales process • Sales presentations Open days Proposals	Deliver brand and product positioning Stimulate interest Inform/educate Inspire purchase Complete sale	Position central messages Tag line	Prospects Customers

Personal selling – Intermediaries Business development force • Sales process • Sales presentations Open days	Raise awareness Reinforce brand and product positioning Stimulate interest Help grow market Support sales efforts	Position central messages Tag line	Intermediaries
Sales promotions • Introductory offers • Discounts • Trialling • POS	Stimulate interest Prompt contact Inspire purchase	Position central messages Tag line	Prospects Customers Staff Intermediaries
Direct marketing • Direct mail • Dimensional mail • Online marketing • Telemarketing • SMS text • Catalogue marketing • Kiosk marketing • Direct response • TV/channels	Raise awareness Stimulate interest Prompt contact Inspire purchase Reinforce brand and product positioning	Position central messages Tag line	Prospects Customers Staff Intermediaries
Events/presence Marketing • Trade shows • "Workplace" • Exhibitions/fairs • Seminars • Open days	Educate/inform Product launch Stimulate interest/leads Prompt contact Inspire purchase	Position central messages Tag line	Prospects Customers Staff Intermediaries
Educational campaigns • Gurus • Technical standards • Universities • R&D	Educate/inform Stimulate interest in the product category need Prompt contact Reinforce brand	Position central messages Tag line	Prospects Customers Staff Intermediaries

Testimonials	Educate/inform Stimulate interest Inspire confidence Reinforce brand and product positioning	Position central messages	Prospects Customers Staff Intermediaries
Web/online marketing	Educate/inform Stimulate interest Prompt contact Reinforce new brand and product positioning Inspire purchase	Position central messages Tag line	Prospects Customers Intermediaries

SUMMARY

In the start up and emerging stage of growth, the venture is all about its new product and pushing it out into the marketplace, seeking the early adoptors and low-hanging fruit as buyers who are much needed for revenues to sustain the business and for reference for other would-be buyers. In the next chapter, rapid growth stage will be seen to depend on shifting the business beyond a product push only focus and onto a market demand and brand position model. How such a business strategy/model is created and the revenue/earnings benefits that accrue are explained.

Chapter 4

Marketing Gearbox: Decisions for Stage Two/Rapid Growth Stage

INTRODUCTION

In this chapter we review three major accelerants of business growth and value creation:

1. Building the corporate brand and associated new product development and customer relationship management processes
2. Developing and managing channels to market, including key account management
3. The process of internationalisation.

RAPID GROWTH STAGE OVERVIEW

Company Characteristics

Sales and customers reach a critical mass. Employee numbers become significant – often upwards of 70 to 100 staff. The company finds a niche, a market, a pattern and a formula for repeat business. Successful business patterns replace *ad hoc* experimentation and not knowing where the next piece of business will come from. Whereas sales was the imperative of the start up and emerging stage, the imperative now shifts towards developing the company's operational infrastructure and the capability to sustain growth as the "hot product" fades and the initial team moves on. As the number of clients, employees and transactions increases, along with organisational complexity, the business must focus on operations and, in particular, must understand which processes are critical to revenue growth. Functional departments emerge, such as finance, marketing, sales, IT, HR and operations/production. Business planning now becomes critical.

Company Goals

- Extend product range, with the second and third new products

- Gain critical mass of customers and revenue
- Organise and structure the business

Marketing Objectives

- Maximise existing market share
- Establish brand position
- Grow channels
- Key accounts and intermediary management
- Enter new markets

Communication Strategies

- Create brand preference
- Encourage wider and more frequent use in existing markets
- Create new markets

Communication Media

- Advertising
- Personal selling/intermediaries
- Promotion
- Publicity

* * *

MARKET INTELLIGENCE

In rapid growth stage, full marketing environment scanning is done systematically. *Focus groups* and *depth interviews* are used to determine customer needs and competitor positions; segmentation research is carried out to position and build a leadership brand in the targeted attractive and profitable customer segments.

Figure 4.1: *Market Research Process*

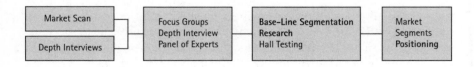

Full needs-based segmentation research is executed at this stage covering seven steps that yield for each market segment found brand positioning, brand purpose and brand value set (see Figure 4.2).

Figure 4.2: *Segmentation Research Steps*

Segmentation Research Step	Key Outcomes
1. Needs-based segmentation	Customers are grouped into segments according to their similar needs and benefits sought in solving a buying problem
2. Segment identifier	Identifiers are established for each needs-based segment, for example demographic, industry category, usage or buying behaviour, etc.
3. Segment attractiveness	Segments are ranked according to predetermined criteria
4. Segment profitability	Profitability (net marketing contribution) is determined
5. Positioning	Based on the segment's unique needs and priorities, the positioning is devised to meet those needs in a differentiated way
6. Test and tune	Test and tune the positioning, using visuals/storyboards in each segment
7. Marketing-mix strategy	Design the marketing-mix strategy to execute the positioning in each market segment

CORPORATE BRAND POSITIONING DEVELOPMENT

Initial Personality Brand

In the early stages of an entrepreneurial venture, the entrepreneur is the brand position and the primary driving force to deliver it. In the served marketplace, they personify the business and its product offer. The entrepreneur lives and breathes the business, and what the business can do for prospective customers, and they will personally engage in significant promotional, PR and sales activity. This creates the initial "personal" brand, whereby market credibility is built through the entrepreneur's expertise, honesty and future orientation.

Figure 4.3: *From "Personal Brand" to "Leadership Brand"*

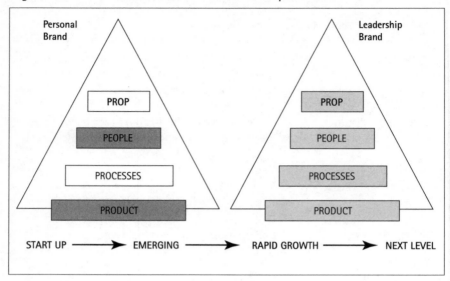

In the start up and emerging growth phase of the venture, significant headway can be made on this basis. However, competing in the marketplace relying only or largely on a personality brand and product (which can be copied by competitors) is not sufficient to bring the business into rapid growth stage.

Significantly scaling the customer base and revenues requires:

1. The research and development of a leadership brand position that represents a compelling idea that captures customers' attention and loyalty by filling an unmet or unsatisfied need
2. Communicating that brand position in a striking, visually distinctive way to the target customer segments and
3. Making an indelible, favourable impression on the customer, using a brand platform that gives clarity of organisation-wide focus and a holistic delivery of the brand position by all people, processes and technologies in the organisation. (This third stage is the key to an entrepreneur's exit at maximum value realisation.)

If you build it ... they may not come

Having a great new product is no guarantee that the target market will beat a path to your doorstep. Think about all of the communication "noise" out there; your target market is bombarded daily with hundreds of visual, textual and auditory messages.

If you build it ... they may not trust you

Moreover, even when they come to your doorstep, would-be buyers have doubt, uncertainty and fear about using a new provider company. Their trust in you has to be earned, for a working relationship to be established and the buying involvement to get underway.

These are the two key business issues that face every entrepreneur and their new product/venture. Branding is the solution. When underpinned by a strong position or customer value proposition, it solves these key competitive challenges. Branding is the way to beckon and to ensure delivery of a customer value proposition, i.e. the whole organisation lives and breathes the position.

Figure 4.4: *Branding as the Competitive Strategy*

Branding beckons

Contribute to shifting products away from commodity price driven

Branding simplifies choice for the consumer in a crowded market

Distinctive Brand

Brand values that mirror customer values foster trust and loyalty

Strong Positioning Customer Value Proposition

A strong brand can force distributors to carry your product

Branded communication can create a sustainable differentiation

Branding creates the compelling and unifying platform for staff to deliver the value proposition

Branding can accelerate entry into related markets

Branding breathes

Brands and Buyer Behaviour

Communicating sameness is a waste; communicating differentiation is the catalyst for growth and success.

Brands work best in markets where buyers have to get involved with the potential seller and product, i.e. they must learn more about a complex product proposition. The buyer can often feel unsure or distrustful of providers. They need assurance about the provider and product credibility. In these *high-involvement purchase markets*, the buyer initially is driven by the need to *learn*, so they can evaluate based on sound information and *feel* assured, before they become comfortable to complete (*do*) a buying transaction.

Brands are also very important in *infrequent purchasing markets*, where the purchase is sizeable and not made very often. Brands provide assurance for buyers in these markets that a wrong purchase/repent at leisure situation will not occur.

Figure 4.5: *Brands and Buyer Behaviour*

	THINK	FEEL
High-involvement purchasing complex, high risk infrequent transactions	Informative (Economic) **Learn-Feel-Do** Expensive cars, appliances financial services	Affective (Psychological) **Feel-Learn-Do** Expensive cosmetics, jewellery, fashion clothing
Low-involvement purchasing simpler, low risk frequent transactions	Habitual (Responsive) **Do-Learn-Feel** Consumer goods, petrol	Satisfaction (Social) **Do-Feel-Learn** "Life's little pleasures" (Beer, cigarettes, sweets)

A brand position becomes the shorthand for a consumer in these markets, shortening the consumer's learn time and maximising their feel of assurance about the purchase. Over time, the brand comes to encompass all of the positive and negative associations, perceptions and experiences that an interested (or potentially interested) consumer has about the company and its brand position. The sum total of these will define the brand's equity or value for the consumer. Where brand equity or value is high or higher than competing brands, then the consumer will always include it in their purchase consideration set. According to McKinsey & Co., the top three brands in a consideration set will secure as high as 70 per cent of the sales opportunities in a market. For those brands placed fourth or lower, the opportunity for sales falls to 40 per cent.

How the customer comes to have those associations and perceptions about a brand is influenced significantly by how it is presented to and talked about in the marketplace, the specific expectations that are created in the customer's mind and as promoted by the organisation's brand proposition communications, and finally by how the customer actually experiences the brand. Assuming a compelling customer idea or value proposition exists, branding is effected by:

- Communication tools, such as advertising and PR, which are the primary creators of the brand position awareness and initial expectation.
- The early stages of the sales process, informational brochures and interactive media, such as the web, then explain the brand position more fully and convincingly. They secure customer comprehension

of the brand's differentiation and relevance to their key needs.

- Completion of the sales process and service and account-handling interaction through ongoing customer relationship management conclude the delivery of the brand position and, crucially, underpin the customer's confidence for its future usage and in their recommending it to friends and colleagues.

Leadership Brands

Leadership brand positions are built over time in a very specific progression of four consumer perceptions: differentiation, relevance, esteem and knowledge.

Figure 4.6: *How a Leadership Brand Is Built*

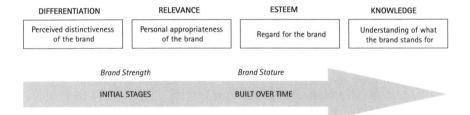

Differentiation

This is the foundation stage and it is when great brands are born. Differentiation is the brand's ability to stand apart in the market and is the extent to which it is perceived as being unique, different and distinctive. Without this foundation, a brand will not survive as the market evolves.

Relevance

This is about how appropriate the brand is to the target customer's wants and needs. Without broad relevance, a differentiated brand may be a niche brand.

Brands that achieve high levels of both differentiation and relevance can lead or even define a category and thereby strongly contribute to operating income. The next two foundation blocks to high brand equity are esteem and knowledge, which in combination define brand stature. Leadership brands excel in both brand strength and brand stature.

Esteem

This is about how good a target audience feels about a brand and comprises quality and popularity as the critical dimensions. Being held in esteem helps a business cope with downturns and bad times.

Knowledge

The market knows and understands what the brand stands for, what the company's products and services are and knows the positioning, promises and values of the brand. This is the result of all communication and experiences that the market receives over a period.

Brand Position Development Process

The initial product-led phase must be replaced by a market-led brand strategy in the rapid growth stage. The entrepreneur must therefore implement and manage the key strategic marketing process of developing a differentiated, relevant brand position that over time is held in esteem and known for its values. The objective should be to achieve brand strength through initially securing a differentiated and relevant position and then gradually adding brand stature.

In broad terms, there are three phases to brand position development: the research and analysis stage, the position development stage and the strategic brand communication and implementation stage. All three phases require a considerable management top team involvement and commitment to the outcomes.

Template 10: *Corporate Brand Position Development Process*

Inputs	Process Step	Output
Existing brand perceptions in key target groups Definition of desired position	**Brand review**	*Gap analysis* Summary of current brand status versus desired brand status
Market analysis Competitor analysis Customer value analysis	**Current situation analysis**	*Summary current position* • SWOT • PEST • Brand hypothesis
Current brand status Desired values and utilities SWOT Brand hypothesis	**Brandstorm**	*Definition of brand task* • Definition of gap between desired and current • Plugging the gap • Implications

Brand hypothesis Delivery capability Competitive brand positions (Ireland and overseas)	**Proposition development**	*Concept proposition* • Market position • Ethical and emotional values • Brand personality • Target market
Company brand proposition Competitor propositions Concept boards Identity Delivery examples Product specifications	**Proposition validation (branded product research)**	*Proposition definition* • Key elements • Preferred verbalisation • Fit with products • Expectation of delivery
Branded product propositions Proposed delivery plan	**Proposition refinement**	*Refined proposition* • Specific value • Brand personality

Branded product propositions
Proposed delivery plan
	**Implementation plan
	"brand beckon"
	"brand breathe"**
		*Communication and
		experience programs*
		• To be translated into
		  creative work and media
		  selection
		• Touch points in sales and
		  service

Source: pFour Consultancy and the author

Research and Analysis Stage

Brand Review

The starting point in the process would be interviews with key managers (in marketing, customer service, sales, production, finance) and with agencies responsible for the previous corporate design and advertising to determine:

- Brand development and values to date
- Existing brand perceptions by staff, consumers, intermediaries and stakeholders
- Current brand delivery: to what market segments, levels of customer satisfaction and associations held with the brand
- Current brand communication executions: advertising, literature, point of sale, consistency of message, visual identity, style, tone, product specifications/design documents, advertising/image tracking data, customer service guidelines, staff training materials and competitor literature/advertising/websites.

Brand Status

From the information and views gathered in brand review, a working document would collate the following:

- Brand values analysis, to capture those that are perceived, variations by audience, potentially differentiating brand values and brand fit with the business vision and strategy
- Market analysis, to assess market trends that may impact upon the brand and to learn from any exemplars
- Competitor analysis, to determine current and likely future activity
- SWOT analysis of the business and its marketing environment
- PEST analysis, to scan for issues and implications
- Target audience definition.

At the end of the research stage, the team will have: reviewed how competitors position their brands; identified what market/PEST trends may impact the positioning development; looked at the business strategy/goals and how the brand aligns; and gathered the views of staff, managers, customers, etc. on current and desired brand values. This working document drives the "brandstorming".

Position Development Stage

Brandstorm Session(s)

In one or more sessions with key managers and agency suppliers, the group works to create and define three to five credible, motivating and differentiating brand positionings and to estimate the scale of the task to achieve each one. The group would:

- Review gaps between the current brand positioning and that identified as desired. What are the functional values? What are the emotional values?
- Review the gap between the desired image (to go with the desired brand positioning) and current image delivery. What implications are there for product range/delivery, customer relationship management, channel strategy and staff/training?
- Consider implications for customer communications.
- Develop the three to five brand positions.

Positioning Interrogation

The emerging brand positions along with imagery and preferably new product concepts and customer relationship propositions that align with the positioning, go into depth interviews and focus groups for interrogation.

Example 4.1: *Brand Positioning Used in Research for a Financial Services Company*

Company XXXXX — Listen. Advise. Deliver.
Company xxxxx is the financial planning company that gives you advice you can trust so that you can make choices with confidence.

- We listen to your situation and questions and give you straightforward and honest information on a whole range of financial issues and products.
- We use our financial expertise to help you gain financial peace of mind.
- We will not sell you anything you do not need and you can trust us to deliver on what you do need.

Positioning Refinement and Validation

At the end of the focus-group research, the brand positioning would be benchmarked against key competing brands, analysed for uniqueness/ sustainability and assessed against the business delivery capability/ change implications.

Example 4.2: *Research Feedback and Analysis on a Brand Positioning (not Complete, to Protect Confidentiality)*

Overall Motivation	Key Deliverables	Positives Honesty
• Positive reactions • Answers major concerns	Local offices Knowledgeable staff	**Negatives** Too good to be true
Verbatims		
"... not out to con you ..."		Type of company people, products not geared to a specific product range
		Target market "All ... anybody"

Base-Line Segmentation Research

Customers are grouped into profitable, attractive and identifiable segments.

Brand Implementation Platform

Brand Beckon and Brand Breathe

Following the needs-based segmentation research and position definition work, the brand position is then translated into the set of key customer brand values. These values will guide how all staff, processes and technologies are engineered to deliver the brand position – in effect the set of levers or shorthand to guide all management decisions and business strategy. In addition to assuring consistent and continual delivery of the "brand breathe" (i.e. the whole organisation lives, breathes and delivers the brand position to customers), the values will also guide the creation of the "brand personality", which in turn determines the creation of an intrinsically striking brand that makes an indelible impression on the customer mindset.

Figure 4.7: *The Brand Implementation Platform*

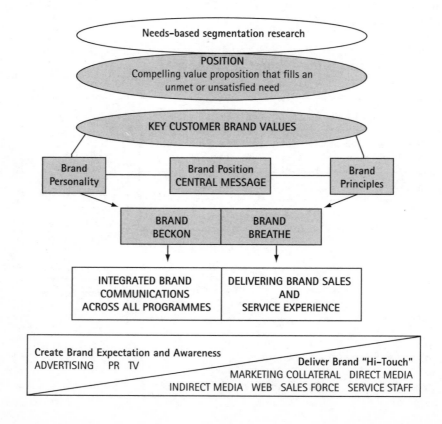

Brand Beckon: Brand Personality and Communications

Brand Beckon

The shaded elements of the brand platform in Figure 4.8 are used to develop and decide on the brand beckon communications programmes.

Figure 4.8: *Brand Beckon Communications*

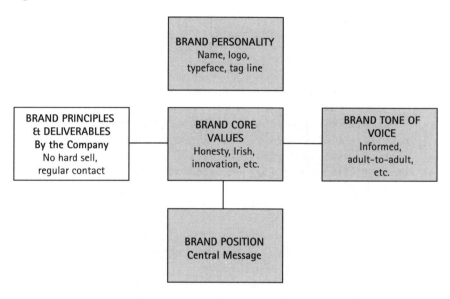

Template 11: *Advertising Agency Creative Brief and Media Planning*

Project Name: Billing Code:
Client: Requirement:
Date: Deadline:

Creative Development

1. Brand position statement:
    Product category:
    Target audience:
    Unique benefit:
    Importance to customer:
    Difference to competitors:
    Why should target audience believe you?

2. What situation has created a need for this communication?
3. Explain the service, product, offering, concept or point of view the advertising needs to address.
4. What is the one thing you want your target audience to believe about your product, service or point of view after seeing this communication?
5. What competitive advantage does the firm own that proves this one thing?
6. What do you want your target to feel, think or do because of the advertising?
   Feel:
   Think:
   Do:

Media Plan Development

If a media plan is required, questions seven to ten must be answered.

7. Which target industries are key to your business? To which industries are you most interested in talking? Which have the biggest impact on your business?
8. Timing and seasonality are two related but discreet entities. Timing refers to the length of the advertising period (for example, fiscal year versus calendar year), whereas seasonality refers to times during the year when advertising becomes more or less important (for example, perhaps summer is slow, therefore not a high priority).
   - What is the advertising period?
   - Is there any seasonality or are there times of the year when it would be more important to be advertising?
   - Are there any trade shows or conventions that need to be supported with media (for example key magazine issues, etc.)?
   - Does advertising need to support the business on a global, national or local basis?
   - If advertising needs to support the business on a national basis but has a priority in a specific region, which regions are important?
   - What are the criteria for market selection (for example sales volume, competitive pressure, sales development, etc.)?
9. What are the key market areas?
10. What is your budget for advertising?

Brand Experience Delivery Programme

The brand experience programme has to be developed and implemented if the "beckoned" customer is not to be disappointed. Particular attention has to be paid to the hi-touch points of interaction between the customer and the brand promise. If a powerful position is vital for a strong differentiated brand, then ensuring that the business and its key processes (marketing, sales, service, etc.) are aligned and dedicated to delivering the brand position and brand personality is crucial to ensuring it lives and is experienced by the customer – consistently and continually.

Figure 4.9: *Brand Breathe Delivery*

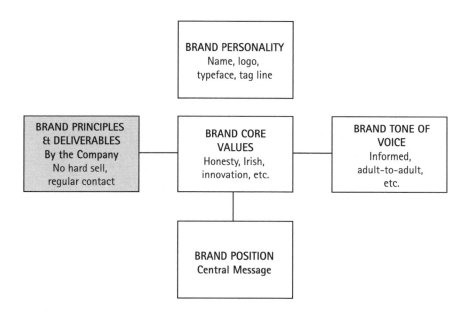

PRODUCT POSITIONING DEVELOPMENT

After the initial product-led phase of emerging and the early rapid growth stage, the business will look to

- Expand sales of existing product to existing markets – this is the *market saturation objective*
- Expand sales of existing product to new markets – this is the *market extension objective* (internationalisation, stage 1)
- Create new sales from new product to existing markets – this is the *market penetration objective*
- Create new sales from new product in new markets – this is the *market extension objective* (internationalisation, stage 2).

* * *

Template 12: *Corporate Brand Position Experience Programme*

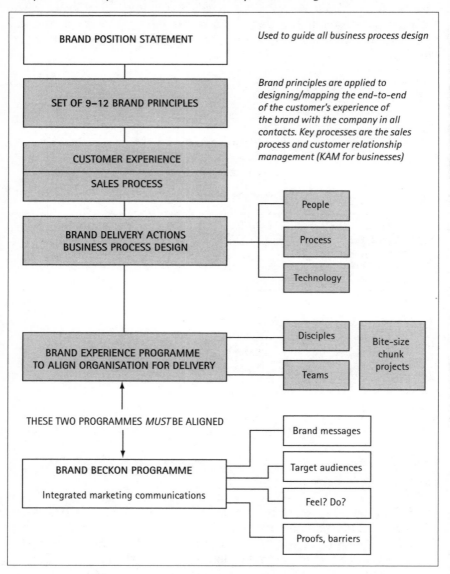

Adapting existing product to enter new markets and creating new products becomes a key strategic marketing process to be managed in the business. Here are the stages in the *new product development process* (and/or product adapt):

Internal Management Review

This is the start point, with depth interviews with managers in marketing, customer service, sales, production and finance – and with partners, intermediaries, alliance members – focussing on their views, perceptions, thoughts and ideas on:

- The current product(s), types and the rationale for their development to date
- Target markets, market definition and segmentation
- Perceived strengths and benefits, weaknesses and opportunities
- Pricing policy, profitability
- Methods of product distribution
- Sales support and promotions
- Unexploited skills, resources, technology, other assets
- Sales trends
- Product literature – for each stage of the sales process.

Market Screening

Desk-based research of the product category to identify:

- Key trends and developments
- Critical success factors
- Products marketed.

Product Screening

Review products in other relevant markets to identify potential unique features and benefits of possible relevance:

- Product literature review
- Product features
- Specific targeting
- Product linkage
- Product positioning
- Distribution and sales support
- Advertising and promotional materials.

Example 4.3: *Product Screening Information for a Financial Services Product (Detail is excluded to preserve confidentiality)*

Product XXXXX	
Product positioning	
Core features	
Additional benefits/options	
Specific targeting	

Pricing	
Product linkage and packaging	
Sales channels	
Product literature evaluation	
Overall assessment	

Gap–Opportunity Analysis

A working summary document to capture learning to date under the headings of:

- Current products versus competitors, evaluation
- Review of strengths and weaknesses
- Identification of opportunities and threats
- High-value/unique ideas and features for incorporation in product development and positioning
- Prioritisation and principles for future product development.

Product Concept Generation

Create outline product specifications using the guiding principles and criteria of market-area utilities, key customer needs/values, fit with corporate brand, sustainable competitive advantage, ability to deliver and projected long-term market direction.

Figure 4.10: *Product Concept Elements*

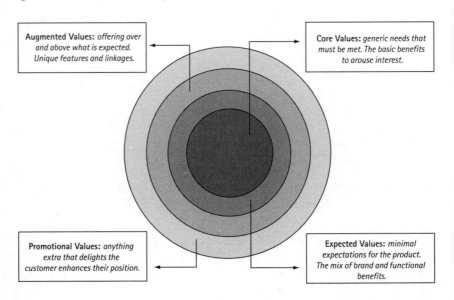

Figure 4.11: *How Consumers Value a Service*

How do consumers value an intangible purchase of a service?

Consumers buy three types of service:
1. A convenience service is typically inexpensive. It is a recurring need and consumers do not particularly care where it is bought. There is no involvement with the seller. For the seller, generally, price and distribution channels are the key marketing mixes to focus on in these markets. (For example, newspaper delivery service.)
2. A shopping service requires more buyer involvement with the seller. The buyer gives more thought; they want to compare options and look carefully at price, quality, style and image. For the seller, promotion is they key marketing-mix element to focus on, particularly brand. (For example, designer clothing retailing service.)
3. A speciality service is purchased infrequently, has high involvement for the buyer and requires time and effort to get right. For the seller, promotion and a credibility brand are the key marketing-mix elements to focus on. (For example, mortgage or financial advisory service.)

Consumers value a service in four dimensions:
1. **Form** – the way the service is delivered
2. **Place** – where the service takes place
3. **Time** – availability when needed
4. **Possession** – ease of acquisition. Quality, Price, Guarantees.

Testing of Product Concepts

The product concepts are then put into focus-group and depth-interview research, comprising a mix of existing and target customers. Areas of discussion and probing include:

- *Current product category holdings*, perceived needs, triggers for purchase, evaluation criteria
- *Attitudes to providers*, perception of brand(s) and values, relevance and importance of values
- *Response to branded product concepts*, evaluation of features, product likes and dislikes, strengths and weaknesses, brand fit, expectation of price/value
- *Response to communication and channel mechanisms*, expectation of where and how to get advice and buy advice/service/relationship expectations.

Product Interrogation

The findings of research are then incorporated in further refinement of the product concepts and a panel of experts is recruited to "interrogate" the products for market saliency. The panel (commentators, journalists, analysts, etc.) offers:

- Perspective on future market trends, competitor and product trends
- Perspective on targeting
- Evaluation of the product concepts
- Potential gaps and areas of opportunity not currently addressed.

Competitor Benchmarking

In addition to the panel assessment, key competitor products would be benchmarked – using competitor product literature, published materials and so on:

- Mapping of new product(s) against competition
- Feature-by-feature comparisons
- Strengths and weaknesses
- Identification of USP/positioning
- Accept or reject decision on each product concept.

Base-Line Segmentation Research

The accepted product concepts are put into segmentation research to assess levels of demand, interest by segment and delivery expectations.

Impact Assessment

Product, channel and customer segment information is then reviewed against production resource/investment requirements.

Business Case

A business case for proceeding with product production would then be made. Headings would include:

1. Executive summary and brief overview of the case purpose and desired outcome
2. Current situation – factors and reasons for proposed product
3. Fit with business mission, strategy, goals and brand
4. Industry and market assessments *vis* the product
5. Competitive and competitor analysis

6. Product description
7. Project proposal
8. Resources required
9. Financials – P&L estimates, cash flow, balance sheet impacts, capital cost
10. Implementation
11. Risks
12. Recommendations
13. Appendices.

PRODUCT ADOPTION

In the rapid growth stage, the challenge in securing adoption of a radical/new product is to bring the early and late majority buyers (34 per cent each) on board.

Figure 4.12: *Product Adoption*

Target Group	Early Majority *Pragmatists*	Late Majority *Conservatists*
Focus	A proven product that lowers cost/gives competitive advantage	Help to sustain competitiveness
Characteristics	Not risk taker Likes to work with market leaders Wait-and-see attitude Does not like surprises	Resistant to change Risk averse Price sensitive
Needs	Complete solution Needs credible reference Customers in their industry	Simple solutions Wants to buy established standard
Role in adoption process	Entry point into huge mainstream market	Significant market Can be quite profitable

Source: Derived from Figure 4.4, "Key Characteristics, Needs and Role of Adopter Groups" in Adrian Ryans, Roger More, Donald Barclay and Terry Deutscher *Winning Market Leadership, Strategic Market Planning For Technology-Driven Businesses,* John Wiley & Sons Canada Ltd 2000

Template 13: *Product Positioning Development and Launch Process*

Process Stage	Inputs	Outputs
1. Internal review	Internal interview and review focusing on: • corporate objectives • project objectives • development rationale • target markets • market definition • market segmentation • SWOT • pricing • distribution • unexploited technology • sales	Clear direction on research scope and expected outcomes
2. Market screening	Desk and on-site research in leading countries/markets covering: • review of key trends and developments • competitive environment • legislative and regulatory • technology developments • critical success factors	Contribution to definition of likely future state
3. Product screening	In-depth examination of market leading products, using desk research, on-site and associates covering: • product literature • product features • targeting • product linkage • product positioning • sales mechanisms • sales channels • promotional	Identify unique features and benefits relevant to NPD objectives
4. Gap/opportunity analysis	Collate, review and distil information into a working summary document. Key headings to include: • market projection(s) • current product strengths, weaknesses, opportunities and threats • gap identification • high value/unique features for incorporation • prioritisation for future product development	Definition of future opportunity and success factors for product development
5. Product concept generation	Using the working summary documents, develop outline product specifications against key criteria: • market area utilities • customer needs/values • strategic fit with brand/progression • achieving sustainable competitive advantage • ability to deliver • projected long-term market evolution	Outline branded product propositions constructed in levels: Core: generic need that must be met/basic benefits Expected: minimal expectations beyond basic Augmented: offering over and above what customer is accustomed to and has in expectation terms

6. Product concept validation	Group/depth research to test • current product holding • perceived needs • hierarchy • purchase triggers • evaluation criteria • knowledge of area • attitude to providers • current provider • their brand/values • relevance • response to product concepts • evaluation of features/benefits • likes/dislikes • versus current products available • strengths and weaknesses • expectation of price/value • response to communication mechanism • expectation of how/where to purchase • level of advice/info/service expected	Recommended product propositions and key success features for: Innovators – Early adopters Majority – Laggards
7. Product interrogation	Taking the product specifications developed from the research findings, convene and facilitate a *panel of experts* to thoroughly probe for market saliency. Using authoritative sources (industry experts, journalists, players) in one or two interrogation sessions to: • evaluate and refine the product concepts and targeting • develop revised/refined concepts for quantitative research	Final product concepts ready for quantitative research
/competitor benchmarking	Benchmark against the major competitor's products: • mapping against competition • feature-by-feature comparison • strengths, weaknesses • potential USP/positioning • accept/reject option	
8. Full segmentation research	Covering the following areas: • product options • delivery options • target market characteristics • target market needs	Quantification of target segments, including ranking of segments and definition of product and delivery specification
9. Impact assessment	Detailed impact assessment for the new products and their delivery to the different segments. Outline: • resource requirements • investment requirements • delivery requirements • time-frames	Resource and profitability impact assessment, including critical success factors
10. Business case development	Business case for new product "go": • detailed product description • brand positioning • communication programme • detailed costings • sales revenues projections • capital costs	Approval of new product for development and launch

CHANNEL MANAGEMENT

Key Account Management for Critical Customers

It is an immutable business fact that 80 per cent of revenues come from 20 per cent of your customers. It therefore pays to focus on those key customers. Key account management (KAM) is one of the best ways to ensure repeat purchases, additional purchases and referral to other prospective customers. Would it not be great to have new customers like your best existing customers?

So how does it work? It starts with the dedication of a key account manager whose role is to lead and manage the key account process. How the key account sees the role of the manager is of major importance. The key account will expect the manager to:

- Be the main link into your company for all issues
- Understand its business, market needs and competitive environment
- Help sell them products/services that achieve their business objectives
- Add value in the relationship to their business by, for example, advising on issues relevant to their business
- Help exploit market opportunities and identify new challenges
- Act with integrity and professionalism.

Four Levels of Relationship

There are four levels of how a key customer may currently perceive your business in relation to theirs. KAM is needed to shift perceptions from a commodity or product supplier – and its implications in terms of price sensitivity and loyalty – to a value-add and partner relationship.

Figure 4.13: *Relationship Levels with Key Account Customers*

Perceived Level	Customer Response	Solution
1. Commodity	High price sensitivity No loyalty	Differentiate/add benefits to product to get to level 2
2. Product provider	High price sensitivity Low loyalty	Understand customer aims and support some of them. Stage 1 of KAM process
3. Value-add	Less price sensitivity Some loyalty	Stage 2 of KAM process Stage 3 of KAM process Stage 4 of KAM process
4. Partner	**Low price sensitivity** **High customer loyalty**	**Full KAM process**

KAM has four stages:

Template 14: *Key Account Management*

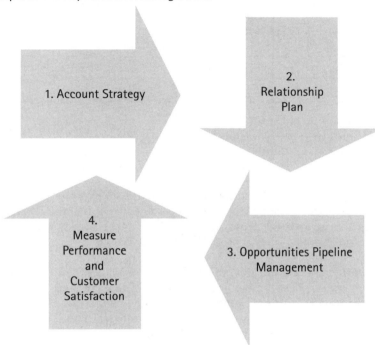

Account strategy: developing a *customer-account-specific* sales strategy that is based on the customer's agenda of issues and needs. A well-developed strategy will address:

1. What you can do to add value for the customer
2. Who you need to influence and by whom in your company
3. Where within the customer organisation to target
4. When to pursue opportunities
5. Why the customer will buy from you.

Complete an account strategy charter for each key account, starting with an understanding (using secondary research, see Chapter 2) of the accounts industry and current situation. Ask the account for their key business objectives for the next three to five years and what they critically need to do to achieve those objectives. Ask how you can help them to achieve their objectives.

Figure 4.14: *Devising a Key Account Strategy*

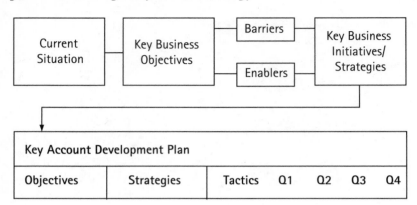

Information collected and analysed is then translated into an *account development plan*, which sets out your objectives for the year, the strategies that are to be deployed to achieve those objectives and the quarterly actions or tactics that execute those strategies.

Relationship plan: identifying the key decision makers who are in the customer's power base and who make things happen, and devising a *relationship development plan* to provide value to them at a personal/social and business level. A good understanding of the key decision makers will address the following questions:

1. What is their business agenda?
2. What is their personal/social agenda?
3. By whom do they need to be recognised?
4. How are they measured?

Complete an organisational map of the key account, identifying the power base (power base decision makers, PBDM, and influencers, PBI), the supporter base sponsor (SBS) and anti-sponsors (SBAS).Then decide your *mirror-relationship team* alignment pairings – CEO–CEO, CFO–CFO, etc.

Opportunities management: managing the *pipeline of opportunities* from initial identification to qualification and go/no-go decision and then from pursuit/closing to final contract and engagement.

With the account development plan (objectives, strategies and tactics) and the organisation relationship map (target audiences) in place, a programme of interaction and communication can begin through hospitality, contributing to the account's internal newsletter or staff conference, industry conference, seminar/briefing for the account top team on relevant industry issues.

Figure 4.15: *A Key Account Organisation and Relationship Map*

CEO	
PBDM	SBS

CFO		COO		CIO	
PBI	SBAS	PBI	SBS	PBDM	SBS

Performance/satisfaction measurement: survey, interview and early warning flags to measure and track your account performance and the customer's satisfaction.

For each key account, an annual performance measurement and customer satisfaction survey should be carried out as a precedent to updating the account development plan and organisation relationship map.

Figure 4.16: *KAM Performance Measures*

Key Measure	
Opportunities	Review of opportunities identified, qualified, pursued
Sales	Targets, achieved and forecast
Relationships	Strength of interpersonal, mirror-relationship
Satisfaction	Buying process and moments of truth
Alerts	Symptoms of potential retention issues

Intermediary and Re-Seller Business Development

Many businesses have to deliver their product in whole or to a significant degree through "channels" that they do not own or directly control. As businesses with such channels to market move beyond the start up and emerging stage, a dedicated marketing strategy and process needs to be developed to achieve rapid growth and then proceed to next level stage.

The key process steps to developing a marketing strategy to maximise business through an intermediary/re-seller channel are as follows:

Current Situation Analysis

Using internal and external sources, information is collated and analysed across the following areas:

- Company total revenues and trends by intermediary channel type
- Company product revenues and trends by intermediary channel type
- Company share of total intermediary channel type market
- Intermediary channel type profiles and segmentation
- Key company financial data by intermediary channel type, for example repeat business, persistency, support (sales and servicing costs)
- Market drivers, issues and opportunities impacting the intermediary channel types.

Internal Interviews

These are a series of interviews with a cross-section of staff with perspectives on different areas of dealing with the intermediary channel types and cover the following areas:

- Current understood intermediary channel strategy
- Historical evolution of the intermediary channel types
- Strengths and weaknesses of company channel management
- Opportunities, options for future channel management
- Threats to channel going forward
- Plans for development and organisational implications
- Perceptions of: intermediary segments; intermediary needs and preferred relationship features; intermediary customer types/segments; and relevance of corporate brand to intermediary decision making/product recommendation
- Potential areas of competitive advantage to focus on.

Intermediary Interviews

Intermediary interviews are a series of depth interviews amongst a representative sample of intermediary channel types to ascertain their needs, their customers' needs, their perception of intermediary segmentation, the role of brand in their decision-making process, their basis for product recommendations to customers, their preferred generic product characteristics and their views on potential areas of competitive advantage. Gaining an understanding of their attitudes to suppliers is a potential segmentation base for competitive advantage. Use questions such as the following:

- Whom do they use and for how long have they used them?
- What are their evaluation criteria for using suppliers, probing: levels

of support, relationship, service, brand, product, knowledge/advice, technical, marketing and staff?

- Do they perceive any current suppliers as having a clear strategy and plan to work with the intermediary channel?
- How is this manifest?
- If categorising suppliers, how would they do so? Rank them.
- Who is poor and why?
- Are differences between suppliers very significant? If so, what are these significant differences?
- What are the characteristics of suppliers who work well with intermediaries?
- Complete the supplier ranking map:

Figure 4.17: *Intermediary Ranking Map of Suppliers*

Area of Importance	Your Company	Competitors		
Understands the business Strong personal relationship Excellent service Good product range Good remuneration Good sales support Knowledgeable staff Easy to do business with Other				

Brainstorm Session

Taking the learning from internal and external research, the group validates and adapts the emerging "intermediary segmentation" and develops a series of brand/concepts that represent your company's desired position and best meet the intermediary channel type's needs.

Example 4.4: *A Financial Services Intermediary Segmentation (showing two types, without compromising confidentiality)*

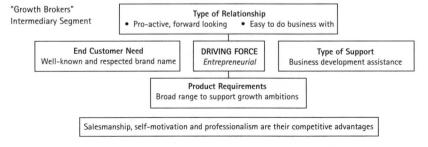

119

Intermediary Brand Concept Testing

A sample of the emerging intermediary segments is then researched with a series of four or five branded concepts to determine appeal and segment coverage.

Example 4.5: *A Financial Services Intermediary Branded Concept and Segment Response*

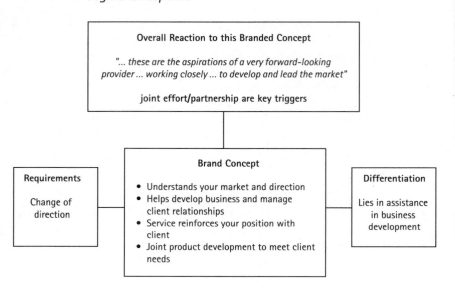

Brand Implementation

Having confirmed the brand concept that appeals to the key intermediary channel types and the areas of differentiation to focus on, you must now begin the final stage: identifying the cultural, structural, technical and marketing/sales requirements that are needed to communicate and deliver the brand experience.

Template 15: *Intermediary Corporate Brand Positioning Development Process*

Process Steps	Inputs and Analysis	Outputs
1. Current situation	Collation, review and analysis of: current channel position, strengths and weaknesses, opportunities and threats, intermediary perceptions, needs, motivations, competitors, best practices and exemplars ...	Overview of current situation and scoping/identification of key enquiry areas and issues
2. Exemplar reviews	Desk-based review to identify best practices and learnings	Intermediary models and key learnings

3 intermediary interviews	Initial segmentations used for interviews with intermediaries on market needs and inter-supplier comparisons	Development/validation of existing segmentations. Gap analysis. Intermediary assessments of suppliers, their preferences for brand, product and service
4. Expert panel	Opinions and views on evolution of intermediary/channels	Test/validate possible intermediary strategies. Likely evolution of channels
5. Brainstorm	Create and interrogate propositions and key components for the intermediary channels	Outline propositions for brand, product and service
6. Research	Concept propositions researched in group and depth interviews	Refined propositions for each segment

Source: pFour Consultancy

INTERNATIONALISATION

The Process

In the late emerging stage/early rapid growth stage, the business starts its internationalisation, frequently by "passive/indirect exporting", whereby multinational businesses in the local market and visitors will buy the product for consumption back in their parent country/country of origin. Thereafter, the journey can evolve as follows:

Figure 4.18: *Process of Internationalisation*

	Indirect Export	Agents/Partners	Multi-country	Global
MOTIVATION	Opportunistic	Sales volume	Sales volume Risk diversification	Scale Share value
ACTIVITY	Reacting to enquiries	Selling through agents' partners	Source internationally Foreign subsidiaries JVs, alliances	Global
PERSONNEL	No one dedicated	Hire international sales manager	International team	Multinational
CAPABILITIES	Domestic focus	Develop export capability	Multi-currency Overseas manufacture	Multi-country capability

Export Readiness

The International Trade Centre has a very useful export readiness diagnostic/checklist that scores the resourcing, competitiveness and expectations dimensions of readiness once you have answered questions on:

- Your business/current position

- Your product/service/competitiveness
- Export objectives
- Management team/support
- Market-entry strategies
- Export motivation
- Your industry
- Promotional approach
- Relevant experience.

A lack of readiness in one or more of the above areas will signal remedial or further preparation in some or all of the following key success factors:

- Hire staff who are familiar with your target market
- Senior managers must be willing to travel frequently to meet potential customers
- Develop/attain an internationally recognised quality assurance system and service quality standard
- Train staff in the culture and customs of your target market
- Start with a market that is predisposed towards your product/early adopter
- Consider entering the market with a local partner
- Talk to foreign customers in your local market about their country-of-origin market
- Talk to foreign alumni of your alma mater in your local market about their country-of-origin market
- Talk to other national companies operating in the foreign target market.

International Market Research

Research is the key first step in targeting the right (first) market to enter. In addition to sales potential, other aspects such as infrastructure availability, levels of competitor activity and stage of product adoption are key enquiry areas. Market intelligence is built using the secondary research and primary research techniques and sources set out in Chapter 2, albeit now for foreign markets. Legal, financial and accounting advisers will also be key providers of information.

Gather information and data on the following for the target country:

- Economic trends
- Political environment
- Currency rates
- Foreign investment and approval procedures
- Restrictions on termination and non-renewal

Template 16: *International Expansion Strategy Development*

MANAGEMENT	FINANCE	COMPLIANCE
Roles and responsibilities	Grants/supports	Accounting and audit
Structure of operations	Funding through revenues, debt	Corporate, personal, indirect
International teaming	and equity	and property taxes
Information systems	Partnerships and distributors	Intellectual property protection
	Acquisitions in target market	Transfer pricing
	Currency management	Profit repatriation

- Access to resources and raw materials
- Availability of transportation and communication channels
- Labour and employment laws
- Technology transfer regulations
- Language/cultural differences
- Access to affordable capital and suitable sites for units
- Government assistance programs
- Customs, laws and import restrictions
- Tax laws and applicable treaties
- Repatriation and immigration laws
- Trademark registration and protection
- Costs and methods of dispute resolution
- Agency laws and availability of appropriate media for marketing efforts.

New International Market Entry

Market entry strategies favoured are to select a first-priority region, secure initial business revenues and then focus on building operations there, rather than trying to expand into all regions at once. This is termed the win-and-build approach.

Indirect export marketing, using foreign subsidiaries located in the local market as network facilitators and/or product buyers is an entry strategy that quickly builds foreign market buyer trust and brand familiarity. Similarly, using introduction by professional services networks can accelerate successful market entry.

Product will require adaptation to meet local marketing, regulatory and technical requirements. Marketing, sales and service materials and manuals, agreements and so on will have to be internationalised. Make sure your product name, slogans and concepts "translate" in target countries and cultures. For example, Coca Cola's launch name in China translated into "female horse stuffed with wax".

Template 17: *Product Adaptation for International Markets*

Product Adaptation, Management and Implementation Process	
Stages	**Example Activity**
1. Secondary research	• Government, trade and information databases for target country • That country's companies in your local market • Fellow national companies already in that target country
2. Primary research	• Mystery shop analysis via trade fairs • Depth interviews, initial focus groups
3. Gap/opportunity analysis	• High value/unique features identification • Short/medium/long-term development prioritisation
4. Initial concept/product screening criteria go/no-go	• Initial concept screening criteria (examples below) are used to include/exclude features

Criteria	Description
Fit with your brand	• Consistent with brand values • Enhances overall brand amongst target audiences?
Fit with existing product range Relative profitability level	• Perceived to add value to current offering • Minimises risk of product cannibalisation • Achieves minimum required profitability targets • Potential to generate additional cross-sales
Degree of competitive differentiation	• Establishes a clear positioning for company in the marketplace • Not regarded as "me-too" by consumers and distributors
Level of competitive insulation	• Not easy for the competition to match it easily or quickly • Maintains a competitive edge for company as long as possible
Speed of implementation Relative flexibility	• Ability to bring new products/services to market • Ease of upgrading or amending to suit changing consumer/commercial requirements
Perceived customer value	• Meets (and exceeds) customer's expectations • Customer unable to obtain better value for the same cost

| | Synergy with existing systems and capabilities | • Ease of development and implementation by the company
• Cost of acquiring necessary capabilities |

| 5. Concept/product next stage development (staff) | Build out the complete product specification | • Internal (staff storm sessions) |

| 6. Concept/product next stage development (experts) | • Panel of local and international experts to participate in a "delphi" research and development process | |

| 7. Concept/product next stage development (consumers) | • Qualitative research (focus and depth interviews)
• Quantitative research (market sizing) | |

| 8. Product/concept refinement | • Good bits, bad bits, improve its
• Core, expected, augmented own promotional values | |

| 9. Priority/implementation | • Feature(s) decision | |

| 10. Product "introduction file"/ launch file and specification | • High-level product concept, positioning (seller, intermediary, partner and consumer) features and benchmarking | |

Pricing
• Features/costing/assumptions

Process
• Systems spec
• Administration
• Documentation
• Training
• Compliance
• Service levels
• MIS reports
• Translation process

Promotion
• Key customer/seller/intermediary/partner elements/messages
• Communication strategy
• Communication mix
• Customer sales and service literature
• Information literature
• Training sales process
• Data/database etc.

Place
• Trialling
• Sales process design
• Sales budget
• Launch/training
• Campaign management
• Competitor reaction/assessment etc.

Think Global — Act Local

Take account of the local business etiquette, culture and norms. Be global, but act local. For example, American customers are receptive to new ideas, innovations and change and the bottom-line is an all-embracing driver. Conversely, German buyers are cautious, risk averse and driven by product quality and customer satisfaction. Clearly, the failure to recognise these differences in your marketing communications would be detrimental.

Aaron Marcus and Emilie West Gould ("Cultural Dimensions and

Global Web User-Interface Design: What? So What? Now What?" http://tri.sbc.com) examined dimensions of culture, as analysed by Geert Hofstede in his seminal study of cultures in organisations, and considered how they might affect user-interface designs for the web. They find that different cultures look for different data to make decisions. Sacred colours in the Judeo-Christian West (red, blue, white, gold) are different from Buddhist saffron yellow or Islamic green. Subdued Finnish designs for background screens might not be equally suitable for the USA.

Geert Hofstede researched employees of IBM in 53 countries and highlighted essential patterns of thinking, feeling and acting. His five dimensions of culture provide a significant insight and framework for interaction with consumers and buyers in these 53 countries.

Figure 4.19: *Cross-Cultural Communications: Differences that Influence Marketing Communications and Selling Actions*

1. Power–Distance Culture Dimension

This refers to the extent that less-powerful members of a society expect and accept unequal power distribution. In high-PD countries, you see centralised political power and tall hierarchies in organisations. There are "bosses" in business, teachers are esteemed and parents value obedience. In low-PD countries, there are flatter hierarchies, people are more equal and equality is expected.

High Power Distance: Malaysia (104) Arab Countries (80) India (77) Brazil (69) Hong Kong (68)
Low Power Distance: USA (40) Canada (39) Netherlands (38) Australia (36) Ireland (28)

2. Individualism versus Collectivism

Individualism in cultures implies loose ties; everyone is expected to look after themselves/their family and no one else. Collectivism implies people are integrated into strong, cohesive groups that protect in exchange for loyalty. Individualistic cultures value personal time, freedom, challenge and extrinsic motivators such as material rewards at work. In family relations, they value honesty, truth and maintaining respect. Individual socio-economic interests are above that of group, maintain strong rights to privacy and emphasise ideologies of self-actualisation. Collectivist cultures value training, physical conditions, skills and the intrinsic rewards of mastery in the workplace. In the family, they value harmony more than truth/honesty; they use shame to achieve behavioural goals and strive to maintain face.

High Individualism: USA (91) Australia (90) Canada (80) Belgium (75) France (71)
Low Individualism: Arab Countries (38) Hong Kong (25) Chile (23) Costa Rica (15)

3. Masculinity versus Femininity

In terms of gender roles, in masculine cultures, the traditional roles are strongly maintained – assertiveness, competitiveness and toughness. In feminine cultures, the home/child orientation and tenderness roles are apparent. Masculine culture work goals include earnings, recognition, advancement and challenge. Feminine culture work goals include good relations with all colleagues, good living and working conditions and employment security.

High Masculine: Japan (95) Austria (79) South Africa (63) USA (62) Arab Countries (53)
Low Masculine: Israel (49) France (43) South Korea (39) Netherlands (14) Sweden (5)

4. Uncertainty Avoidance

People vary in the extent that they feel anxiety about uncertain or unknown matters (as opposed to fear of an actual threat). Cultures vary in their avoidance of uncertainty, creating different rituals and having different values regarding formality, punctuality, legal/social/religious requirements and tolerance of ambiguity. High uncertainty-avoidance cultures have more formal rules in work, require longer career commitments and focus on the tactical, rather than the strategic. They tend to be expressive; people gesticulate, raise voices and show emotions. People expect structure to make events clearly predictable. What is different is perceived as a threat. By contrast, low uncertainty-avoidance cultures focus more on long-range, strategic goals in work. They are less expressive. People seem easy going and relaxed.

High Uncertainty Avoidance: Belgium (94) Japan (92) Chile (86) Mexico (82) Brazil (76)
Low Uncertainty Avoidance: Canada (48) UK (35) Ireland (35) Hong Kong (29) Denmark (23)

5. Long versus Short-Term Time Orientation

Long-term time orientation cultures have been influenced by Confucian philosophy, with beliefs around unequal relations being key to a stable society, the family as the prototype for all organisations, and consequently older people have more authority than younger, and virtuous behaviour in work is about acquiring skills and education, working hard, being frugal, patient and persevering. This plays an important role in Asian countries. Western countries were by contrast more likely to promote equality, individualism and fulfilment through creativity and self-actualisation.

High Long-Term Time Orientation: China (118) Japan (80)
Low Long-Term Time Orientation: Poland (32) Germany (31) USA (29) UK (25) Pakistan (0)

Source: Geert Hofstede (1991)

Doing Business in...

Conducting business face2face varies from country to country. The following provides guidance for selected economies around the world.

Figure 4.20: *Doing Business in the USA*

The USA offers a marketplace of 290 million people. According to Enterprise Ireland's *Starting Up and Marketing in the USA – A Guide for Irish Technology Companies* (http://www.enterprise-ireland.com), successful Irish entrepreneurs rate the following promotional tools as being the most important in selling industrial goods and services in the USA:

- *Personal selling*, through a direct sales force and/or through intermediaries.
- *Sales promotion and incentives*, with three key tools: pitches/presentations, brochures and a website. Many companies deeply discount on initial key customer orders to establish "reference" in the market.
- *Trade shows* are regarded as one of the most effective strategies.
- *Lead generation and direct marketing to target*, qualify and initiate contact.
- *Public relations*, to build the personal and company brand in the target market.

Many Irish entrepreneurs select one of their own executives to re-locate to the USA and manage the key process of building the sales infrastructure. Salaries vary widely according to role, location and experience, but a senior sales manager can expect to earn a base of $85,000–$150,000 with an aggressive commission structure and an employee package of health insurance, employee share option scheme and 401k retirement savings plan.

The business culture in the US is open and innovative, and requires a mirroring sales approach. Business people tend towards a direct, informal, optimistic and vocal style of communication. Key cultural and business norms are:

- Prior appointments are necessary and punctuality is expected. Business breakfasts are common, as are working lunches.
- Business meetings happen in almost any context and situation, and business people are direct.
- Almost all business is conducted in English.
- Most US executives will be uncomfortable standing with less than two feet between you both.
- The culture stresses individual initiative and achievement and the concept of "time is money" fosters quick and decisive decision making. They value straightforward and to-the-point information. Americans tend to be future oriented and innovation is therefore embraced.

- Money is the key priority, with lesser importance attached to status, protocol, national honour and social niceties.
- Many multicultural environments are encountered.
- Meeting formalities – agendas, non-disclosure agreements, etc. – are considered important. Participants will get down to business after a small-talk period to break the ice. This will not cover personal matters but rather sport, the weather or a light business topic.
- Americans regard negotiating as problem solving through give and take. Often, they will try for an oral agreement at the first meeting. Immediate follow-up is expected.
- US companies typically introduce legalities at an earlier stage of discussions than their Irish counterparts.
- Pricing is discussed early and in detail.
- For a first meeting, dress conservatively and thereafter follow your American counterparts. Business attire is formal on the east coast and tends to be smart casual on the west coast.

Acting like a US company – "act local" – and appreciating the business norms and culture are key to success. Two practical adaptations for this are:

1. Establish a ".com" website rather than a ".ie" (Irish domain address) and use a short, direct word.
2. Titles are different in the US for Senior Positions, so use the US position titles on your business cards. For example "President/CEO" for "Managing Director", "Chief Marketing Officer" for Marketing Director and "Vice President Sales" for Sales Director.

Source: Enterprise Ireland, *Starting Up and Marketing in the USA – A Guide for Irish Technology Companies*

Figure 4.21: *Doing Business in Japan*

The Japanese market is significant, with over 127 million people. It is quite unlike the markets of Europe or the USA. It is a very different culture: personal and business relationship are established and maintained in ways that are different to the West; decisions take longer; formality and politeness are key; and roles played by employees can be unexpected of their "title".

Key business and cultural norms are:

- Deeply conservative ethos, yet embracing of innovation. In retail markets, pioneer brands are very highly favoured.
- Strong commitment to education and work.

- Many Japanese values are based on religious beliefs that emphasise the maintenance of harmonious relations with others through membership in a family and a community. This leads to an emphasis of community over the individual person.
- Trust, co-operation and loyalty are fostered by harmony and completeness in a community or group and this in turn yields business success.
- Confrontation and argument tend to be avoided, so projects and business proposals are seldom discussed openly in detail by a group. Instead, decision making is undertaken with a *Nemawashi* (project champion) and a *Ringi-sho* (proposal process).
- Initially, the project champion will informally brief and explain what they are planning to propose formally to key decision makers in the company – seeking understanding, advice and comment. This avoids "surprise", which can lead to a proposal decline.
- After this, a written proposal is circulated among all persons whom it may affect. Those who approve it, affix their seal to the document and pass it to others of equal or higher rank. Eventually, it is brought up through management to the board of directors. At this stage, proposals are usually approved for implementation.
- Few Japanese are sufficiently fluent to conduct business comfortably in English, so it is important to translate all documentation and work with translators.
- Because of politeness, the Japanese will generally not wish to offend by saying they do not understand; you must therefore ask for clear feedback at every stage.

According to Enterprise Ireland's *Doing Business In Japan – A Guide for Irish Technology Companies*, Japanese contacts will expect to be provided with a lot of detail about you and your company. The following material should be provided *before* the meeting:

- Corporate brochure, introducing the company and stating the company mission, product expertise and USPs
- Profiles of company management
- Your client base
- Your partner companies
- Your financial backers
- Current trends in your industry and where you are positioned
- Case studies of your product
- Reasons why your product should be used/the value proposition
- Visual explanation and illustration of how your product works.

Source: Enterprise Ireland, *Doing Business in Japan – A Guide for Irish Technology Companies*

Figure 4.22: *Doing Business in Western and Central Europe and France*

With 290 million people and 20 per cent of world trade, Continental Europe is a bigger market than the USA or Japan. Europe leads the world in many sectors, with dynamic market growth in informatics (B2B e-commerce market projected to reach $1.4 trillion in 2005), pharmaceutical, medical, biotechnology and financial services.

There are many markets and opportunities to consider. You will reach 70 per cent of the Western European IT market by concentrating on three areas: the UK, France and the German-speaking countries of Germany, Austria and Switzerland.

Amongst the opportunities noted in Enterprise Ireland's *EUR-Open for Business: A Presence in Europe* guide are:

- Niche opportunities exist to supply agricultural equipment to Central Europe's largely underdeveloped agricultural sector. Poland is rated as a high opportunity.
- A feature of the Central European and Russian regions catch-up in technology is the lack of legacy equipment and opportunities exist in computer hardware sub-sectors such as credit card readers, internet kiosks and smart card infrastructure.
- Opportunities exist for e-learning and e-government, particularly in Hungary and Russia.

Doing Business in France

Key business and cultural norms are:

- Make appointments for both business and social occasions. You will not be considered late if you arrive ten minutes after the scheduled time.
- France practically shuts down in August.
- Staying late in the office is common for senior executives.
- The best time to schedule a meeting is usually 11 am or 3.30 pm.
- The way you dress will be perceived as a reflection of your social status and business success. Wear only conservative clothing of the highest quality.
- Most business people read English, so there is no need to have your business card translated into French. However, it is strongly recommended that you learn basic French phrases and use them whenever possible – your efforts at this will be appreciated and remembered.
- French business people tend to focus on long-term objectives and will try to establish firm personal relationships.
- During a first meeting, remain polite and cordial. A carefully planned, logically organised and structured proposal is key, as logic and analysis will drive the French negotiators.
- You will be judged on your ability to demonstrate your intellect and this will often

involve discussing confrontational ideas and rigorous debate. How you perform is the key.

- Digressions in the middle of a debate are characteristic. Every detail is pored over, so decisions can be lengthy affairs.
- The workplace is highly structured and hierarchical; bureaucracy and administration procedure are considered more important than efficiency and flexibility. Change is not necessarily embraced and risk-aversion is common.
- Power is intrinsic to the business culture; only the highest-ranking individual makes the final decision.
- Despite the formality, people tend to stand close when speaking to one another and touching a shoulder is within the bounds of etiquette.

Source: Information on doing business in France was derived from the www.executiveplanet.com business culture information series and was contributed by Maurice Contal, Director of the Cross-Cultural Management Consultancy Firm – World Executives

Figure 4.23: Doing Business in Germany

Key business and cultural norms:

- Arriving fifteen minutes late could be fatal to a potential business relationship.
- Germans are not usually comfortable with discussing serious business matters "on the go", so be prepared to make appointments – even for a detailed telephone conversation. Breakfast meetings are not part of the culture.
- The preferred time for meetings is between 10 am and 1 pm and between 3 pm and 5 pm; avoid Friday afternoons. Germans commonly take lengthy holidays in the July/August period, in December and over the Easter period.
- Formal, dark and conservative suits are the norm in corporate business and banking.
- Small talk is not a significant social function in the German culture. The German culture is highly fact oriented. Mingling is not customary.
- German companies compete in a rigorous but not ruinous way. They share market share, not domination. They despise price competition and instead compete on the basis of excellence in their products and services.
- The German manager wants the best product for his company – product quality and customer satisfaction. The key words/motivators are quality, responsiveness, dedication and follow-up. German managers expect to inspect a plant's production line and processes. A third objective – after quality and service – is co-ordination with government, particularly on standards, policies and regulations. Virtually all German products are subject to "industrial norms".
- Managers are not driven by short-term bottom-line results. Their style of management is collegial, consensual, product/quality oriented, export conscious, loyal to the company and committed to its long-term prospects.

- In very formal meetings, the highest-ranking person enters the room first. Rank and status are determined by achievement, not age. Germans like to learn as much as possible about your background and qualifications from your business card. Expect them to address issues, problems and facts through very technical communication behaviour.
- Agendas will be followed. Objective facts and legalistic rational reasoning will underpin negotiations.
- German managers are cautious of new ideas and concepts and do not respond to the "sell" as other risk-takers do.
- When preparing promotional and presentation material, be aware that German business people are traditionally less impressed by glitzy advertising, illustrations and slogans. Brochures aimed at the German market are often more serious in tone, provide substantially more technical product data and support claims with hard facts and examples.
- Decision making is slow, protracted and every detail is examined

---

Source: Information on doing business in Germany was derived from the www.executiveplanet.com business culture information series and was contributed by Alexia and Stephan Petersen who serve as consultants and trainers to a wide spectrum of companies and non-profit organisations on the topic of intercultural communication. www.aspetersen.com

Translation Tips

1. Translate only relevant sections of documents, having consulted clients and sales teams.
2. Take the burden off words – use images, pictograms and diagrams where possible.
3. Be clear about documents that are "for-information" and those that are "for-publication": they require very different levels of translation support.
4. A press release is not a website; a sales brochure is not a user-manual. Style, pronunciation, word choice, phrasing and sentence length will vary depending on where the text appears and what you want it to achieve.
5. Check what language the reader speaks – British or American English?
6. Check local typographical conventions: in German, nouns take capital letters; in Spanish and French, months and days of the week do not take an initial capital.

International Market Development

Try closing the first clients quickly by making deals as attractive as possible for them; they will serve as references for others. When others sign up, you can begin marketing and adding staff. In terms of a foreign market presence, you can do business direct, through a local presence or through distributors/intermediaries.

- **Case for direct:** particularly if distributors will not provide your optimal care for customers.

- **Case for distributors:** particularly if it is a market where they will only buy from fellow nationals (for example Japan).

- **Case for local presence:** markets such as the USA want to see commitment before customers trust the new company.

Buying the right local company can really speed up entry and growth in a new market – to add a new product, technology, service or customer segment. Review qualifications and credentials of possible partners; get help from overseas credit bureaux, industry associations and commercial attaches. Always ask for multiple references. Try to build a trial period into the contract – to cover due diligence.

The management team and their location are a key consideration. Some recruit locally and functionally direct from the home market. Others encounter difficulty recruiting locally and have to locate a senior team member in the overseas market. Many do locate a senior execute in the overseas market. Few have top marketing teams that include executives from the various countries in which they do business. Only some have effective processes for knowledge transfer across countries. Miscommunication problems can arise, so do exchange teams to spend time in one another's shoes and get people together regularly to exchange ideas.

INTEGRATED MARKETING COMMUNICATIONS

In the rapid growth stage, all elements of the integrated marketing communications programme are deployed – including sponsorship.

Sponsorship

Good sponsorship(s) helps a company build relationships, brand and new business. Most organisations will run a significant sponsorship to reinforce its core message to the marketplace.

Below is a series of key tests to apply in considering a sponsorship. A vital one is the extent to which the company can and is allowed/facilitated to network and leverage audience contacts.

Checklist 4.1: *Deciding a Sponsorship Involvement*

1. Relationships (importance weighting — 42 per cent)
- Audience
  - Will it draw the right audience?
  - % clients attending from previous years
  - % targets attending from last year

- Networking
  - Passes/discounts for company people
  - Are co-sponsors targets or clients?
  - Are there hospitality events for networking?
  - Can we add/customise such events?
  - Can we add on customer contacts pre-/during/post-event?

- Programme
  - Do program producers provide quality sponsor service?
  - Previous sponsor references
  - Profile of past audiences provided
  - Past attendees' evaluations

2. Brand (importance weighting — 33 per cent)
- Positioning
  - Does programme theme support the company's core message to market any exclusivity opportunities for the company?
  - Are we in a "leadership" position as sponsor?

- Association
  - Are presenting speakers/other sponsor brands the type with whom we want to associate?
  - Is there a limit to premier sponsors?
  - Is there a limit to all sponsors?

- Visibility
  - Does it include company visibility to the marketplace pre- and post-event?
  - Does it include on-site visibility?

3. Business (importance weighting — 25 per cent)
- Demonstrate services
  - Opportunity to demonstrate company services
  - Opportunity to demonstrate company materials

- **Business development**
  - Is there sales process/support in place to drive/leverage leads at pre-/during/post-event?
  - Can we get pre-event enquiry and registrant lists?
  - Can we get post-event registrant list with CRM-suitable information on it (for example, registrant's interest areas/openness to further information/etc.)?

In undertaking "sponsorships", it is critical to budget at least twice the sponsorship cost in an additional "promotional budget" that leverages and amplifies the sponsorship.

As the business moves from emerging stage into rapid growth and challenges for next level, the brand position statement will incorporate adjustments based on the market analysis and strategy development for all new channels and for internationalisation.

Template 8: *Corporate Brand Position Statement – To Drive All Marketing Communications (by Channel and Country) – During the Rapid Growth Stage*

Brand Values of the Company	Existing	Desired/New
What are the key "values" held by customers, staff, suppliers competitors and influencers about the company?		
• existing		
• desired/new …		
Key Customer Needs and Values		
Describe the "desired" or expected "needs" under each of these four key dimensions of the "customer buying experience".		
1. Service experience expectation, the key "moments of truth" when it would be delivered and ranking of "moments"	Service Experience and "moments of truth"	
2. Sales experience expectation from how they would become aware of the product, channels through which they	Sales Experience	

would become knowledgeable about its
benefits to them, have questions dealt
with and action a purchase

3. Product features and benefits that meet   **Products**
   and/or exceed their key needs in the
   product category and that are not
   delivered by competitors

4. End goal statement of the customer,   **End Goal**
   setting out in a sentence or two what
   economic social, personal objective they
   will achieve with the product.

Key Message(s)

What are the key brand positioning messages
to be used in all marketing communications?

- brochure/collaterals
- web
- publicity
- exhibitions/events
- direct marketing
- personal selling
- promotions
- sponsorship
- advertising (print, radio, TV, outdoor,
  cinema, channels, SMS, PDAs)

Key Target Customers   **Primary**

Who are the primary target customers
(clients and prospects)? Describe by way of
demographic, geographic, industrial,
personal, purchase attributes, etc.

Secondary

Describe them by reference to their
segmentation profile and descriptor variables
– grouping together segments with similar
requirements and buying characteristics.

Product Unique Selling Proposition	The USPs
The unique benefits offered that • meet the following key customer needs and values • are also different to (or not offered by) the competition • are perhaps sustainable advantages/not easily copied.	_____ _____ _____ _____ _____ _____ _____
Key Interest by Customer Segments Which products or customer needs are specific to the different customer segments?	_____ _____ _____ _____ _____
Differentiation How is the company brand/product different from those of the key competitors?	_____ _____ _____ _____

Template 9: *Corporate Brand — Integrated Marketing Communication Programme for Rapid Growth and Next Level Stages*

- **Marketing objectives:** maximise existing market share. Establish brand position. Grow channels. Key accounts and intermediary management. Enter new markets.
- **Communication strategies:** create brand preference. Encourage wider and more frequent use in existing markets. Create new markets.
- **Priority communication media:** advertising, personal selling/intermediaries, promotion and publicity.

Activity	Role	Key Values/Initiatives	Audience
Brand – corporate • Name • Logo • Identity	Brand position	Position tag line Culture consistent Channel consistent	Prospects Customers Staff Intermediaries Influencers
Literature • Sales guides • Sales brochures • Sales information • Corporate	Build trust and credibility Reinforce brand and product position relevance	Position central messages Culture consistent Channel consistent	Prospects Customers Staff Intermediaries Influencers
Advertising • TV • Press • Radio • Outdoor • Cinema	Brand beckon	Position central messages Culture consistent Channel consistent	Prospects Customers Staff Intermediaries Influencers
Public relations – consumer	Raise awareness Stimulate interest Reinforce brand position Inform/educate	Position central messages Culture consistent Channel consistent	Prospects Customers Staff Intermediaries Influencers
Public relations – trade	Raise awareness Reinforce brand position Educate/inform	Position central messages Culture consistent Channel consistent	Prospects Customers Staff Intermediaries
Sponsorship	Raise awareness Reinforce brand position	Education/product category needs awareness Culture consistent Channel consistent	Prospects Customers Staff Intermediaries
Personal selling Direct sales force • Sales process • Sales • Presentations • Sales pay	Deliver brand and product positions Stimulate interest Inform/educate Inspire purchase Complete sale	Position central messages Culture consistent Channel consistent	Qualified leads Prospects Customers
Personal selling – Intermediaries Business development force • Sales process • Sales • Presentations • Sales pay	Raise awareness Reinforce brand and product positions Stimulate interest Help grow market Support sales efforts	Position central messages Culture consistent Channel consistent	Priority intermediary segments
Sales promotions • Introductory offers • Discounts • Trialling • POS	Stimulate interest Prompt contact Activate purchase	Position central messages Culture consistent Channel consistent	Prospects Customers Staff Intermediaries

Direct marketing • Direct mail • Dimensional mail • Online marketing • Telemarketing • SMS text • Catalogue marketing • Kiosk marketing • Direct response • TV/channels	Raise awareness Stimulate interest Prompt contact Inspire purchase Reinforce brand and product positioning	Position central messages Culture consistent Channel consistent	Prospects Customers Staff Intermediaries
Events/presence Marketing • Trade shows • "Workplace" • Exhibitions/fairs • Seminars	Educate/inform Product launch Stimulate interest/leads Prompt contact Inspire purchase	Position central messages Culture consistent Channel consistent	Qualified leads Prospects Customers Staff Intermediaries
Educational campaigns • Gurus • Technical standards • Universities • R&D	Educate/inform Stimulate interest in the product category need Prompt contact Reinforce brand	Position central messages Culture consistent Channel consistent	Prospects Customers Staff Intermediaries
Testimonials	Educate/inform Stimulate interest Inspire confidence Reinforce brand and product positioning	Position central messages Culture consistent Channel message	Prospects Customers Staff Intermediaries
Web/online marketing	Educate/inform Stimulate interest Prompt contact Reinforce new brand and product positioning Inspire purchase	Position central messages Culture consistent Channel consistent	Qualify leads Prospects Customers Intermediaries

SUMMARY

Success in building the corporate brand and channels to market and entering new international markets will dictate whether the venture now goes beyond the rapid growth stage of evolution. These are the essential foundations. In the third stage of evolution, the business venture now adopts formalised strategic marketing planning, regularly reviewing its business positions in the different international market segments and investing/divesting accordingly.

Chapter 5

Marketing Gearbox: Decisions for Stage Three/The Next Level Transition Stage

INTRODUCTION

By this stage – for many, it is some five or ten years after start up – the venture has developed many new products and entered a number of key international markets. It becomes essential in aiming for next level/transition to do a health check of the current product markets. Businesses use portfolio-planning tools to weigh up the relative attractiveness of investing in strategic business units. One such tool is the Directional Policy Matrix (DPM), which can help the management team to build periodically an overview of the business's market positions, assess cash-generating and cash-using products/markets and make strategic decisions on future resourcing.

Clearly, the absence of a strategic review of a current portfolio of products and markets can lead to faulty decisions being made on resources, which in turn will undermine the business's ability to transition with changing market positions.

NEXT LEVEL TRANSITION STAGE OVERVIEW

Company Characteristics

At this point, one of three things happens: the business plateaus, reaching its own internal limitation to growth; the company slowly deteriorates as it clings to old formulae for doing business in a changing market; or the company experiences a breakthrough by redefining its business strategies, structures and processes. It marks a crossroads, sometimes seeing the founder/entrepreneur moving on. If this stage is managed well, the company begins a new cycle on the growth curve – serving new opportunities for profitability, with less intense competition.

External factors often play a significant role in hurling an unsuspecting company into the transition stage. New competitors, new technologies, new industry formations and changing customer demands can all bring about the growth break. Internal factors can also do it – lack of management depth, with the required professional management experience, in the key marketing, finance and HR positions.

Company Goals

- Move to a new level of growth and success
- Leadership branded position in market(s)
- Full internationalisation

Marketing Objectives

- Strengthen market shares, targeting late majorities and develop/enter new markets

Communication Objectives

- Increase frequency of product purchases
- Create new markets

Communication Media

- Advertising
- Promotions
- Intermediaries
- Publicity

* * *

DPM ANALYSIS

DPM analysis is aimed at determining the appropriate strategic planning goals and the right strategies to achieve those goals across the portfolio of products, strategic business units (SBUs) and markets. In broad terms, the DPM is a framework and process to review the performance and relative potential of each product/SBU/market and to decide which products/SBUs/markets to:

- *Build*/develop further/increase market share of
- *Maintain*/resource to keep the status quo or current market share
- *Harvest*/sell off or withdraw from having squeezed the last potential sales
- *Divest*/drop or exit immediately.

DPM Process

For best results, the DPM analysis should involve marketing, sales and operations managers in both plenary and group sessions. It is very important that all can contribute and thereby all can own the outcomes. In process terms, the DPM analysis involves nine steps.

Template 18: *DPM Analysis Process of Market Positions and Market Attractiveness*

1. Determine "markets"	2. Decide market "attractiveness" factors	3. Decide key success factors for "business positions"
4. Weight and score market attractiveness factors	5. Weight and score success factors	6. Plot results on DPM chart
7. Determine major product/SBU/market	8. Set objectives for achievement of goals	9. Define the key strategies to achieve the objectives goals and strategic goals

(1) Determine Markets

The first step is to define and agree the markets/SBUs/product groups or segments that the business sees itself competing in. This should be heavily informed by the external perception – the customers. For example, in the case of the railway industry in the US market, customers re-defined the market as "transport" when the option of car and air travel became available. Once the markets have been defined, size them in current sales terms and at your future strategic goal date (say three or five years' time).

(2) Decide Market Attractiveness Factors and (4) Weight and Score Market Attractiveness Factors

For each product/SBU/market segment, establish and agree the four key factors that define "attractiveness" relative to the overall market. Then weight their importance and score where these factors are likely to evolve over the planning period. This yields a ranking score, which plots that market on the "attractiveness" axis of the DPM grid (see Template 18). Figure 5.1 is an example of market attractiveness ranking for a financial services product.

Figure 5.1: *Deciding Market Attractiveness Factors for the DPM Analysis*

The factors most important in deciding how attractive a market is	A total of 100 points allocated according to how important each factor is in determining market attractiveness	In the marketplace, as it evolves in the future, is this factor: improving, static or declining?	Multiply the weighting by the score to get the market attractiveness score out of 100
	Weighting	Score	Ranking
Factor	10	0.5	5
Growth rate	30	1.0	30
Market size	40	0.5	20
Profit/margin	20	0.0	0
Competitive intensity			55

(3) Decide Key Success Factors for Business Positions and (5) Weight and Score Success Factors

Decide what the critical success factors are in establishing a strong market position. Again, weight each factor and score it in relation to its evolution over the planning period. This then yields a market position ranking on the horizontal DPM Chart Axis (below). Figure 5.2 shows the market position for the same financial product above.

Figure 5.2: *Assessing Market Position in the DPM Analysis*

Factors important in deciding strength of market position	100 points allocated according to importance of factor	How will factors evolve over the planning period – improve, static, decline?	Ranking for our position is the weighting multiplied by the score	For our top competitor, multiply their weighting by their score
Factor	Weighting	Score	Ranking (1)	Ranking (2)
Product	30	0.5	15	30
Sales process	20	0.5	10	10
Price	10	1.0	10	5
Image/brand	10	1.0	10	10
Customer			0	0
understanding	20	0.0		
Service	10	0.5	5	5
Totals			50	60

Ratio equals 1 divided by 2	0.83	DPM	69

(6) Plot Results on DPM Chart, (7) Determine Major Product/SBU/Market, (8) Set Objectives for Achievement of Goals and (9) Define the Key Strategies to Achieve the Objectives Goals and Strategic Goals

Once each product/SBU/market segment has been scored and ranked, the results are plotted on the DPM chart. According to where each product/SBU/market segment lands in the nine sectors of the chart, there are planning goals recommended for future evolution. Guided by these planning goals, the management teams then set objectives and define strategies to realise those objectives.

Figure 5.3: *Market Positions Mapped in Markets and Strategic Implications*

	Strong	Medium	Weak
High	**Protect Position** • Invest to grow at maximum rate • Concentrate effort on maintaining strong position	**Invest to Build** • Challenge for leadership • Build selectively on strengths • Reinforce vulnerable areas	**Build Selectively/ Withdraw** • Specialise around limited strengths • Seek ways to overcome weaknesses • Withdraw if indications of sustainable growth are lacking
MARKET ATTRACTIVENESS **Medium**	**Build Selectively** • Invest heavily in most attractive segments • Build up capability to counter competition • Emphasise profitability by raising productivity	**Selectivity/Manage for Earnings** • Protect existing • Concentrate resource in segments where profitability is good and risk is relatively low	**Limited Expansion or Harvest** • Look for ways to expand without risk; otherwise minimise resources and rationalise operations
Low	**Protect and Refocus** • Manage for current earnings • Concentrate on attractive segments • Defend strengths	**Manage for Earnings** • Protect position in most profitable segments • Upgrade product line • Minimise resource	**Divest** • Sell when maximum cash can be realised • Cut fixed costs and avoid resource input
	Strong	**Medium**	**Weak**
		MARKET POSITION	

Assuming the product/SBU/market segment lands in the Medium Market Attractiveness and Strong Market Position Box, the planning goals become: heavy investment in the attractive segments, build up ability to counter the competition and raise productivity to enhance profitability. The key objectives will include annual sales and profitability, and market share. The strategies to achieve these objectives that lead to the goals will be focussed on *product* (development and competitive insulation), *sales process* (effectiveness and efficiency), *pricing* (to maximise margin), *image/brand* (competitive insulation and to support premium pricing), *customer understanding* (to accelerate sales process) and *service* (productivity and competitive insulation). These are the factors assessed as underpinning future strength in market position.

The results of this DPM analysis are then incorporated in the business's three to five year plan and the annual business and marketing plan for execution.

ANNUAL MARKETING PLAN

Preparing the annual marketing plan is a *discipline* to ensure that the business stays connected to its markets and that the marketing environment is duly analysed and appraised for both threats to and opportunities for the business. It is also a *road map* for all personnel in the business to follow in terms of the marketing actions that will be implemented to achieve specific, measurable marketing objectives, which in turn lead to sales revenues and give effect to the brand position.

The start point is always market analysis – Where are we now? The relationship between the marketing objectives, strategies and actions required to give effect to the overall business strategy can be illustrated as in Figure 5.1.

Template 19: *Market Plan Document*

Marketing Plan Sections/Content		Number of Pages
Section	Area Covered	
1. Executive summary	Current situation objectives, strategies, tactics, responsibilities, control, budget and other resources	2 to 3 pages
2. Objectives	Mission statement, business objectives, marketing objectives	1 page
3. Current situation	Customer markets, competitors, SWOT, PEST	8 to 15 pages

4. Strategies	Segmentation and targeting, competitive advantage, brand positioning	3 to 5 pages
5. Statement of expected results		1 to 2 pages
6. Marketing mix programmes	Product, promotion, place, price, people, tasks/responsibilities	8 to 12 pages
7. Financial budget		1 to 2 pages
8. Operational implications	Key involvements and dependencies	1 to 2 pages
9. Appendices	Competitor information, background data, research results	Pages as required

Figure 5.4: *Marketing: Objectives, Strategies and Actions*

Where Do We Want To Go? **Marketing Objectives**	*How Will We Get There?* **Marketing Strategies**	*Who Does What? How Long?* **Marketing Actions**
1. Increase market share	Segmentation and targeting	Q1, qualitative research programme by marketing department
2. Expand existing market	Increase frequency of purchases by customers. Open new offices	Sales promotions by the sales team in third quarter
3. Develop new market for existing product	Expand into international markets	Desk research on Mexico in Q2
4. Develop new product for existing markets	Market penetration	New product development (NPD) – panel of experts session in Q4
5. Develop new product for new markets	Market diversification	Seek out partner manufacturer in Brazil Q3
6. Increase profitability of existing business etc.	Marketing audit and analysis – DPM etc.	DPM analysis by top team in Q3 etc.

Template 20: *Marketing Planning Process: Insights, Tips and Templates*

Marketing Audit and Analysis

Current Market and Customer Situation

Definition and rankings of current customers and market segments – key customer values, buying process and needs – trends, issues and changes year on year

Competitor Positions Analysis

Competitor actions, campaigns, positioning and differential advantages – competitor and company brand, image familiarity and favourability analysis

Opportunity/Threats/Strengths/Weakness

Internal strengths/weaknesses across marketing, product development, operations, people, management and company resources – external threats/opportunities arising out of social, regulatory, political, technological, economic and competitors – possible distinctive competencies, differential advantages, positioning and assumptions for strategy formulation

Product Portfolio, Strength and Direction

Market attractiveness and product positions – product life cycles

Market Trends and Market Environment

Projections and assessments of trends in sales, profitability, market size/share, customer numbers and competitor – market specific PEST implications, company specific five forces implications

Secondary Market Research websites ...

Worldchambers.com
Intracen.org
Europa.eu.int
Aseansec.org
Latinnews.com
Tdctrade.com
Jetro.go.jp

Freeedgar.com
Bizminer.com
Marketresearch.com
Askelibrary.com
Tscentral.com

Template 1:
Pest Analysis for Market Drivers and Market Strategy
Template 2:
Market Segmentation
Template 3:
Market Research Process
Template 18:
DPM Analysis of Market Positions and Market Attractiveness

New Customer, Product and Market Research

Secondary research programmes to find out who makes up new target markets, what the customer needs are, who the competitors are, what they offer, potential market size

Primary research programmes to get detailed market information, answer specific buying needs and perceptions questions, establish competitive positioning and factors for strategy

Marketing Strategy – Formulate

Market Segmentation

Group customers into segments that have the same buying issues and needs and identify them by a profile that describes them fully

Market Segment Targeting

Select accessible, substantial and stable market segments for targeting with branded positioning and products

Positioning Statement

For each market segment establish and clearly articulate the differentiated and relevant offer that meets that target audience's needs in a better way than the competition

Marketing Objectives

The specific and measurable market/product objectives in terms of: market penetration (current products to current markets), product development (new product to current markets),

Template 8:
Brand/Product Position Statement: To Drive All Marketing Communications in All Channels and in All Markets
Template 10:
Corporate Brand Position Development Process
Template 15:
Intermediary Corporate Brand Positioning Development Process
Template 16:
International Expansion Strategy Development

market development (existing product to new markets) and diversification (new products to new markets)

Marketing Mix Programmes

Tactical decisions and actions and manipulations to ensure that the *right message* (brand positioning) gets to the *right person* (target audience) in the *right way* (marketing communications and sales) and at the *right time* (highest propensity/time to buy)

Place

The channels and delivery systems through which we reach customers and through which they access us for information, purchase and service/support will be effective and efficient mixes of:
- Direct
- Indirect
- Online
- Sales staff
- Service staff

Entrepreneur Insight
New Market Entry: A Winning Formula
Monica Eisinger, President and CEO, MIND CTI Ltd
(Nasdaq: MNDO and TASE)

Template 4:
Channel Decision Process

Template 14:
Key Account Management

Entrepreneur Insight
E-Business Strategy and the Internet
Angela Kennedy, Business Director, Megazyme
International Ireland Ltd

Entrepreneur Insight
Marketing through a Manufacturer's Representative Distribution in North America
Terence Monaghan, Chief Executive Officer,
BetaTHERM Sensors

Entrepreneur Insight
International Marketing and Expansion:
A "Local Global" Strategy
Mario Moretti Polegato, President, Geox International
S.R.L
Ernst & Young Entrepreneur Of The Year ® 2002 Italy

Promotion

Marketing communications to create brand awareness and interest. Marketing collateral and interactive media to explain the full positioning and convince the sales force. Promotion to ensure satisfaction, buying action and future loyalty/advocacy

- Advertising
- PR
- E-marketing
- Direct-mail marketing
- Telemarketing
- Trade shows and exhibitions
- Sponsorships
- Brochures and collateral
- Sales force
- Sales promotions
- Key account management

Entrepreneur Insight

Partnering – A Driver for Innovation and Growth

Lirio Albino Parisotto, President, Videolar
Ernst & Young Entrepreneur Of The Year® 2002, Brazil

Template 5

Advertising Campaign Planning Process

Template 6

Request for Proposal for Media Relations Services to Company

Template 7

Direct Mail Marketing

Template 9

Corporate Brand: Integrated Marketing Communication Programme

Template 11

Advertising Agency Creative Brief and Media Planning

Entrepreneur Insight

Integrated Marketing Programmes to Create a Top European Brand

Mark Bezner, Joint Managing Director, OLYMP Bezner GmbH and Co. KG

Entrepreneur Insight

Brand Building: Without the Budget

Richard Reed, Co-Founder, Innocent Drinks
Ernst & Young Young Entrepreneur Of The Year® 2003, United Kingdom

Entrepreneur Insight

From a Personal-Based Brand to Leadership Brand Position

Padraig O'Ceidigh, Managing Director, Aer Arann
Ernst & Young Entrepreneur Of The Year® 2000, Ireland

Entrepreneur Insight

Integrated Marketing Communications: A New Corporate Identity that had to Be Born Global

Peter Conlon, Chief Executive Officer, Xsil Ltd

Entrepreneur Insight

Lateral Thinking for Brand Creative

Cormac Hanley, Founder, Oasis Design Group & Yoichi Hoashi; Founder of AYA Corporation

Product

Existing portfolio review and development to deliver the product development, market development and diversification marketing objectives

Template 13
Product Positioning Development and Launch Process

Template 17
Product Adaptation for International Markets

Entrepreneur Insight
New Product Adoption
Gerry McCaughey, Managing Director, Century Homes
Ernst & Young Industry Entrepreneur Of The Year ® 2003, Ireland

Entrepreneur Insight
World-Class Product Development
Martin McVicar, Managing Director, Combilift Ltd
Ernst & Young Entrepreneur Of The Year 2001, Ireland

Entrepreneur Insight
A Winning Product Strategy
Fionan Murray, Chief Executive Officer, Let Systems Ltd

Price

Devising and revising pricing to deliver the brand positioning to the target markets
- Market entry pricing
- Price skimming
- Psychological pricing
- Promotional pricing

Template 12
Corporate Brand Position Experience Programme

People

The people, process and technology structuring that must be done to deliver the marketing planning and marketing mix programme
- Marketing staff
- Marketing services agencies
- Sales staff
- Service staff
- Marketing information system

In setting up your website and maximising its reach, visit these sites:

Inventory.overture.comdmoz.coms
Sales.sitesell.com

Marketing Plan

Template 19
Market Plan Document

ENTREPRENEURS' MARKETING INSIGHTS – WINNING DECISIONS

Fourteen entrepreneurs from Ireland, the United Kingdom, Germany, Italy, Australia and Brazil now contribute their marketing insights across the spectrum of the four key marketing decision areas – market intelligence, brand positioning, channels and communications.

Integrated Marketing Programmes to Create a Top European Brand

MARK BEZNER
Joint Managing Director, OLYMP Bezner GmbH and Co. KG

INTRODUCTION

Notwithstanding a depressed German textile market, Mark Bezner has built the OLYMP brand and experience into the number-one shirt brand in Germany and created the most successful shirt brand within Europe in recent years. Sales have grown to over 3 million shirts a year and revenues have grown from 23.8 million in 1996 to 56.6 million in 2003. Some 3,000 specialist shops carry the OLYMP brand shirt collection in nearly 40 countries, including Austria, Belgium, Denmark, Finland, Great Britain, Ireland, the Netherlands, Norway, Poland, Russia, Romania and Switzerland. In addition, the company has established its own OLYMP stores.

The secret to success lies in the way Mark Bezner brings together the "four P's" of marketing in a relentless, skilled and consistent programme that delivers the PROFIT OLYMP proposition to his retailer network. In summary, OLYMP targets the "easy care" (non-iron and wrinkle-free) market segment with a market leading *premium quality shirt* that is continually aligned with customer fashion expectations and needs. Customer groups most receptive to this value proposition are executives and business travellers (hence the "Miles & More" promotions with Lufthansa and specialist shops) and customers in warm/high-humidity climate countries (hence the entry into United Arab Emirates, Dubai, Bahrain and Oman). The shirts are carefully presented in high-value shop systems in both company-appointed specialist retailers and in its own company retail units. For retailers, the PROFIT OLYMP value proposition addresses a key need: maximising sales, using the minimum of costly retail rental space. Retailers' costs of sales (ordering, stocking, price marking, etc.) are minimised by the OLYMP EDI and NOS supply chain management systems.

PREMIUM PRODUCT

Made out of pure cotton, OLYMP provides retailers with ten convincing reasons and customer selling points for its OLYMP Luxor non-iron city collection shirt:

1. **Non-Iron.** Wash, dry and they are ready to wear. The shirts retain their shape after successive washings.
2. **Wrinkle-Free.** Special finishing that retains a smooth appearance all day long.
3. **100% Per Cent High-Class Cotton.** From Egypt, the cotton is one of the highest quality available worldwide.
4. **Body Temperature Adaptable.** Breathable and moisture absorbent.
5. **Cross Stitch Buttons.** It is virtually impossible for them to come loose.
6. **Cuff Buttons.** For style and perfect fit.
7. **Smooth Seams.** High quality sewing threads and machining
8. **Guaranteed Free from Toxins.** Tested to the strict Oeko-Tex 100 Standard
9. **The Latest Fashions.** Four fashion collections per year.
10. **Guaranteed Prompt Delivery.** Available by return mail.

CUSTOMER FASHION EXPECTATIONS AND NEEDS

The OLYMP Express Programme "NOW" offers its retailers new fashion highlights of the season, four times a year, to refresh and excite the carried shirt range and thereby generate sales for the retailer. Customer needs and fashion expectations are researched at the important international fashion fairs such as Paris and Florence where trends are created. The trends picked up are combined with the creativity and experience of the product management teams to meet the demands of target consumer groups.

"MILES & MORE" AND OTHER PROMOTIONS

In addition to product style changes, several times a year OLYMP boosts retailer sales activity and consumer demand with significant sales promotions. Their core promotional programme is OLYMP's participation in Europe's leading frequent traveller programme by Lufthansa (and its partners in the Star Alliance of airlines). Their collaboration with Lufthansa's "Miles & More" is two way: Lufthansa and its partners offer its travelling customers the OLYMP Luxor shirt for purchase and OLYMP offer customers who buy their Luxor shirt in participating speciality shops 500 "Miles & More" per purchase. At the Dusseldorf trade fair in August 2003, visitors to the OLYMP stand were awarded 1,000 "Miles & More". This will be repeated. There is also an alternative promotional initiative to the award miles.

Figure 5.5: *"Miles & More" Promotion*

SHOP SYSTEMS

Sales capacity and stock turnover is demonstrably increased for those specialist shops that use OLYMP's high value, modular "shop walls" and "shirt presenters". OLYMP jointly funds the cost of the units.

SUPPLY CHAIN MANAGEMENT

OLYMP provides a holistic supply chain management system to its retailers, thereby delivering its "space optimisation concept" and OLYMP PROFIT value proposition. This is how it works. Firstly, manufacturing operations in Rumania, Macedonia, Croatia, Indonesia, The Philippines and Burma are closely linked to the Bietigheim head office, where all development, design, cost control and HR are managed. An Electronic Data Interchange (EDI) system automates order processing and reports every shirt sold directly to OLYMP head office, making it unnecessary for retailers to have costly and time-consuming stocktaking, ordering, goods received and pricing procedures. Secondly, efficient logistics combined with a comprehensive Never-Out-of-Stock (NOS) programme that keeps around 250,000 shirts from the standard range constantly in stock (in a warehouse in Bietigheim) mean that if any products run out, a fresh delivery can be made without delay within 24 hours. Retailers do not have to carry shirt stocks on their premises. Finally, the OLYMP shop units are provided to help increase sales and stock turnover frequency. Putting all these elements together, OLYMP offers its retailers a very efficient management solution to costly space and stocking for sales.

OLYMP can be visited at http://www.olymp-hemden.de

Figure 5.6: *Shop Display*

Integrated Marketing Communications: A New Corporate Identity that had to Be Born Global

PETER CONLON

Chief Executive Officer, Xsil Ltd

INTRODUCTION

Few companies this decade can claim to excite the financier, engineer and marketer simultaneously – Xsil Ltd can! Xsil Ltd was set up in July of 2000 by serial entrepreneurs Peter Conlon and Pat Rainsford, long time business partner and friend. A privately held, Irish company Xsil develops, manufacturers and sells innovative capital equipment in the competitive, complex and near-saturated semiconductor equipment market from its Dublin headquarters. Over the space of a year and a half, core processes were developed, perfected and patented. Conlon is a firm believer in his well-tested business model. Not unlike Druker[1] in the late 1950s, he realised early in his career the value-creation propensity of both innovation and strategic marketing for business. Combining both of these areas, he has built one of Ireland's most dynamic companies and has led a team of ambitious individuals to create truly cutting-edge technology.

Xsil's Integrated Marketing Communications Strategy highlights:

- The importance of a well-planned and co-ordinated global launch
- The challenges of marketing a start-up company and some useful tools of promotion.

Stage 1: Start Up/Pre-Launch Phase (May 2000–March 2002)

Xsil initially employed twelve individuals, predominantly from engineering and scientific backgrounds, to undertake the research and development of its core technology. At this early stage, no specific marketing specialist was involved with the company. The strategic decision was taken to remain "below industry radar" during this important incubation period. There were several reasons for this.

Firstly, the leading semiconductor manufacturers were experiencing problems with the combined demand for increased capacitance coupled with miniaturisation of microchips for consumer electronics. A global race began to tackle this problem by developing thinner components and

---

1. In his 1950s publication "Practice of Management" Peter Druker wrote of a companies activities, ".... marketing and innovation add value, everything else adds costs."

utilising newer materials in the fabrication of chips. Silicon wafers were traditionally used in chip manufacturing. Developments in chip design lead to thin silicon wafers becoming the optimal choice of the manufacturer. There was a continuous drive to develop new and more effective materials to lead the next generations of hi-technology chip design. However, these new materials were not without their own set of problems, which presented new opportunities for equipment suppliers such as Xsil. Without attracting the market's attention, Xsil had spent eighteen months developing a laser-based solution to one of the industry's most prominent and debilitating problems. Thinner and new advanced materials were proving difficult to machine. In the past, manufacturers had satisfactorily used mechanical saws to machine, cut and dice silicon wafers. However, this was no longer going to be the case. Thin silicon chipped under the saw and caused other problems such as de-lamination and cracking of expensive wafers. Equipment manufacturers around the world were desperately trying to develop solutions for this problem but to no avail. Xsil's material and laser scientists had developed a solution without raising competitive attention, avoiding some of the early entry barriers often faced by incumbents.

Secondly, secrecy and anonymity allowed Xsil to generate trade secrets and processes and patent them before competition.

Thirdly, before the official launch Xsil had built up Europe's largest laser labs, staffed with some of the world's most talented and capable laser academics and specialists.

Finally, during this incubation period, Xsil successfully signed strategic agreements with two key customers and its most critical suppliers before competition was even aware of their existence or developed technology.

During this pre-launch phase, Xsil concentrated on building the product and perfecting the technology. The marketing communications of the company lay dormant, save for the branding, which, through a single logo, served a primarily stationery function, i.e. on business cards, letterhead, purchase orders etc. The Xsil logo was grey, dull and boring (see Figure 5.7). However, the business cards were made from thin sheet metal and were shiny and unusual. It was thought that as the company was relatively unknown, this format would be a novel way to plant the Xsil name in the minds of stakeholders. In late 2001, Xsil was finally ready to prepare for its market launch. During this time, an experienced marketer and trade show co-ordinator, Jennie Record, joined the company and her primary role was to oversee and manage the corporate launch. It was decided that the launch of Xsil was to be the single-most important business activity for 2002 and would officially kick-off at the Semicon Munich Industry Trade show in March 2002. Prior to the Munich trade show, advertising agencies were briefed and invited to submit corporate identity proposals for management review.

Figure 5.7: *Xsil Logo, May 2000–Jan 2002*

A NEW CORPORATE IDENTITY

The December 2001 Corporate Identity Brief included the following outlines:

Primary Deliverables

A corporate identity that:

- Effectively communicates Xsil's strengths
- Exudes a look and feel that differentiates Xsil from competition
- Can be applied and extended to all forms of the company's communications.

Scope

The re-evaluation of the logo and design of all marketing collateral, including print, trade show design, corporate videos, slide presentations and the website.

Background Information

The market opportunity and customer opportunity: The decision was taken that Xsil's corporate communications must be vague enough to encompass a breadth of possibilities in order to avoid making a commitment to one specific area or to ruling out business through narrowly targeted communications.

Communication Objectives

While avoiding specifics about technological developments, product details and current customers, the company's primary goal was to communicate Xsil's

- Award-winning innovation
- Corporate stability
- Technological richness
- Limitless capabilities
- Continuous research and development
- Flexibility and quality.

Key Take Away

Xsil is an established company whose technical richness provides limitless capabilities to develop and manufacture innovative laser processing solutions.

Competitive Advantage

Because the categories within laser solution manufacturers are so extensive, listing Xsil's competitors would be futile. Simply put, Xsil's competitive advantages are the points that resonate throughout this document:

- Technological richness
- Wealth of capabilities
- Corporate stability
- Flexibility
- Ability to customise solutions for individual projects
- Experience.

Tone and Manner

- Express Xsil as innovative, mature, professional and experienced
- Simple, conversational language as opposed to being technical or full of "buzz" words
- Personal approach; addresses "You", the customer, partner, analyst, interested party, etc.

Corporate Identity Project Elements

Corporate Logo

Although time and money had been invested in the logo, there was the need to re-evaluate this brand image. The good points were that it looked metallic, modern, hi-tech, applied to a technical company, had Morse code above the company name and appeared to mimic the cuts made by lasers onto wafers. However, it was difficult to reproduce on different media, as it was a solid figure with pieces extracted from it. One suggestion was to invert it, so the logo would be "cut out".

Corporate Colour Scheme

Comparable to the logo, Xsil's colour scheme was to complement the company's characteristics: technically oriented, vibrant, flexible, strong and solid, but not outdated, stuffy or unstable. The metallic coloration of the logo was very modern and hi-tech looking, but should be complemented with vibrant accents. Additionally, the "machine" had already been produced, so colours, logos and icons would have to apply to the machine as well. Prior to proposing a corporate identity, the agency had to analyse the product to see what had already been established. Again, this design was not carved in stone but, as an investment had been made into its appearance, it would be ideal to leverage it.

Graphics and Imagery

Continuing with the themes mentioned above, Xsil required backgrounds, graphics and images for PowerPoint presentations, manuals, signage and printed collateral. These had to reflect the company's vitality, stability, capabilities and technology-driven focus.

Product Brand

Xsil's preliminary product names are "Xise 100" and "Xise 200". There will be families of product lines and each need to have a name. The company name itself, "Xsil", could be played with in order for more leverage. For example, "Xsil" sounds like "exel" or "accel" and could have been turned into "Xsileration", "Xsillence", "Xsilerate", something that supports the strength and ingenuity of the product.

Collateral

In this industry, the most effective way of selling is through presentations, samples and customer meetings. Therefore, literature would not be the primary sales driver. Instead, printed collateral would be used to support sales and to provide generic company information for interested prospects. Xsil required a company brochure, a product brochure, CDs, CD covers and manuals, and these projects would be detailed in a future collateral creative brief. The corporate identity had to be translatable to all printed materials.

Administrative Material

For the office, working onsite and for customer meetings, Xsil had to have corporate administrative supplies. This included pens and notepads all brandished with the company logo, website, contact information (notepads only, due to size constraints) and corporate colours. Xsil also needed new letterhead and envelopes that reflected the corporate identity and outdoor signage at Xsil office locations.

Trade Show Displays

Xsil would launch its new corporate identity at the March 2002 Munich Trade Show. Their booth had to be eye-catching, interesting and make Xsil look like a large and well-established Silicon Valley high flyer, as well as meeting all the previously outlined communication objectives.

Website

While the website was not an effective sales tool, it is a necessary agent in providing information about the company for prospective customers and employees. The information made available would be extremely limited and generic, but enough to promote the company's strengths and potential. This was to be a large project that would be addressed in further, more detailed documents and conversations. Even if still in its infancy, the website had to be live by the end of Q1 2002 – pre-trade show.

Agency Selected

Eventually, and following much evaluation, Baseline, a Dublin-based advertising agency, won the Xsil corporate identity contract. They had three months to prepare all collateral for the official March launch and the Munich Trade show. Xsil had work to do during that time too. To be "born global" they needed to achieve certain standards. They became ISO 9001:2000 certified, implemented top management processes and information systems and signed strategic agreements with customers and key suppliers.

Stage 2: Xsil Launch Phase/Semicon Munich, March 2002 – January 2004

The new marketing collateral received in January 2002 was impressive. Baseline ran with the innovation theme in brochures, corporate presentations and videos. The image of Fillippo Brunelleschi's cathedral was used as an eye-catching piece with the caption, "Enabling a new perspective".

The word "enable" featured significantly in all marketing pieces and later became the Xsil tag line or tag word, as the case may be. The corporate logo changed significantly into what it still is today, as seen in

Figure 5.8. It is colourful, vibrant and many people have commented that they now recognise "X" as the Xsil trademark.

Figure 5.8: *The New Xsil Logo, March 2002 +*

The build-up to the Munich show and launch was huge. A full-page advert was taken out in *Semiconductor International,* one of the industry's widest circulated magazines. This generated much interest, as the industry had previously been unaware of Xsil's existence. The ad carried a simple description of the core business, but only enough to whet an appetite and evoke interest, and, of course, an invitation and booth number for the Munich Trade Show that month. Xsil also promoted their winning of the Irish National Innovation Award in 2001 and advertised for additional staff in international trade and national press.

The Munich Trade Show took place in the Munich Fair Centre, 15–20 April 2002. The Xsil booth (as pictured in Figure 5.9b) was a showstopper. The Xsil website went live on the first day of the show and featured basic company information, the goal at this stage being to network and deal with all enquiries through sales staff so no opportunities would be missed. Larger and more vibrant than all other booths, it attracted huge attention from morning to evening throughout the exposition. The main reasons for this were:

- Interest generated from the magazine advert and general curiosity
- The sheer size and scale of the booth during a period of industry downturn
- The free-flowing Guinness and ample seating at the booth allowed people space and time to rest and network

- The fact that there was a working machine on the booth and explanatory videos of the technology on large plasma screens attracted passers by to stop, watch and learn
- The large X, the huge image of Brunelleschi's cathedral and the booth's general vibrancy and smooth sales staff generated much interest. Xsil positioned itself as a huge global player, yet those "in the know" had no idea who they were!

Figure 5.9a: *Munich Trade Show, Xsil Launch, March 2002*

Munich as a marketing communications strategic move was successful and generated many sales leads. In the months that followed, over 80 two-way non-disclosure agreements were signed with potential customers. Samples came in from all over the world. It was apparent that trade shows were an effective mode of promoting a company in a global industry such as the semiconductor industry and became a regular feature on the Xsil marketing calendar.

Magazine articles such as the one depicted in Figure 5.10 ran in selected industry press prior to shows. Direct customer presentations began and, before the end of 2003, Xsil teams had given over 100 of these eleven-slide corporate presentations, which also included a teaser video.

Figure 5.9b: *Xsil Booth Bar – great networking strategy*

Xsil realised that there were simple and effective ways of getting third parties to promote their brand and a new marketing sub-strategy was drawn up. Xsil was going to let other people promote their achievements. Xsil entered all industry and national awards for which it was invited to apply. Time and effort was taken on entry forms and awards processes. Xsil also spoke at academic and industry events. The company also includes a footer on all outgoing company e-mails detailing recent achievements or awards.

In the 22 months after the launch, Xsil achieved the following:

- Fourteen international trade shows, including locations in Tokyo, Boston, San Francisco, San Jose, Taiwan, Singapore and Korea
- Speaking roles at twelve international industry conferences, including the Nagano Institute of Technology Thin Silicon Wafer Dicing and Chip Handling Technology Seminar in Tokyo, where Xsil was the only non-Japanese invited key note speaker
- Winner of the 2001 PricewaterhouseCoopers National Innovation Award

Figure 5.10: *Source: Semiconductor International Magazine June/July Edition 2003*

- Winner of 2002 European Semiconductor New Company of the Year Award
- Winner of the 2003 Tornado Finance and Community Choice Awards
- Winner of the 2003 Irish Innovation Exporter of the Year Award
- Winner of the Irish Software Association Company of the Year Award 2003
- Winner of the Deloitte and Touche Fast 50 Award 2003
- Runner-up Ernst & Young Entrepreneur of the Year Award 2003

- Xsil carried out a series of open days at their headquarters in early 2003. When executives from the top international technology corporations networked with Xsil over a three-day trip to Dublin, they realised just how global the company had become. A great deal was gained through collaborative efforts over the period of the open days.

Progress to Date

Xsil is now established and considered a large global player and a strong competitor in its application areas. The integrated marketing communications strategy proved effective. Xsil, as of January 2003, had three "fortune 100" customers and had a "first customer meeting to signing of purchase order" average running at sixteen months. This is an impressive reflection on marketing efforts. Potential customer samples are now being sent to the Xsil lab on a daily basis for evaluation. As Xsil grows internally, with a current headcount in excess of 120, so too does its brand equity.

The Future

As the company enters its next stage of development – the growth phase – a new strategy is called for. New obstacles must be overcome. Xsil, having generated a handsome amount of sales leads, is developing its marketing and sales departments and has headhunted industry insiders to spearhead sales in both the USA and Asia. Dick Toftness, former senior Agilent executive, was elected VP of business development in the US and Tom Narita VP of sales in Asia. The marketing budget for the future will focus more on current customer sales leads and promotion of the company to the wider community, i.e. financiers and potential acquirers.

The internet has been detected as a weak point in the marketing communications of the company and much emphasis will be put into developing this medium in 2004. The website will undergo a revamp in February 2004, including more corporate information and additional content. The internet is often the first port of call for customers or potential stakeholders in researching Xsil. A primary goal looking into the future is to have a good presence on major search engines and industry websites.

Xsil intends to publish technical and scientific white papers. Xsil technology is now capable of selling itself and, as outside technologists begin to understand the Xsil processes, the subsequent publication of Xsil capabilities will be a welcome addition to the marketing effort.

Xsil's core product is capital equipment with an average price tag in the region of €1.3 million and, due to the level of secrecy in the industry with regard to purchasing, customer testimonials are difficult to release. It is hoped that this problem will be overcome through the arrangement of additional open days at Xsil where participants will sign Non Disclosure Agreements and other confidentiality agreements.

No single mode of communication could have effectively achieved the marketing goals at Xsil. However, through a well-planned, innovative and integrated communications strategy, Xsil has punched above its weight, successfully launched a new corporate identity, achieved its "born global" and business has boomed.

Xsil can be visited at http://www.xsil.com

New Market Entry: A Winning Formula

MONICA EISINGER
President and CEO, MIND CTI Ltd (Nasdaq: MNDO and TASE)

INTRODUCTION

Founded in 1995, MIND has become a leading global provider of real-time mediation, rating, billing and customer-care solutions for the world's largest communications providers of wireless, broadband, wireline and next-generation communications services. Mobile operators, traditional and NextGen telcos, Internet Service Providers (ISPs), Integrated Communication Providers (ICPs), enterprises, governmental bodies and financial institutions in over 40 countries across the globe use and deploy MIND solutions. With the largest install base of VoIP billing solutions globally, MIND has major telcos such as Verizon and China Unicom as clients. In the enterprise call accounting systems market, MIND's clients include Credit Suisse First Boston, ABN Amro and Deutsche Post. MIND is headquartered in Israel and has offices in the United States, Europe and China. The company employs over 180 people worldwide and reported revenues of nearly $4 million in Q4 2003.

WINNING FORMULA: UNDERSTOOD CUSTOMER NEEDS, PRODUCT EXCELLENCE, EASE OF ADOPTION AND PARTNER BRAND HALO

MIND started in 1995 with solutions for corporate customers and private switches call accounting and developed expertise in rating and mediation. More importantly and at the same time, they learned about the needs of communications services providers. In 1997, MIND looked for the entry to a larger space, with more recognition for their state-of-the-art technology. They found a market need for real-time billing in the IP Telephony area and thus found the "entry" point to the profitable, growing and large billing space.

Understood Customer Needs

Billing software is among the key requirements of any telecommunications service provider's systems. It enables the service provider to track and bill for usage and to manage revenues, customer relations, marketing programs and rate plans. MIND was amongst the first entrants to this market space, as most billing vendors had not yet met the technical demands of the dynamic environment of Voice over IP (VoIP) based services.

Product Excellence

With its advanced software capabilities, its flexibility and cost-effective product-based solution, MIND penetrated the billing market that was dominated by giants with high-cost customised projects by offering the "pay-as-you-grow" business model.

VoIP technology required real-time interfaces with network elements for both pre-paid and post-paid services. The larger billing vendors had billing systems that worked in a batch mode, collecting records and periodically generating invoices. These solutions were project oriented and not product based. For pre-paid services, most of the systems were provided by hardware vendors. MIND's solutions were product based, enabling real-time billing for both pre-paid and post-paid subscribers and were pre-integrated with the leading VoIP equipment vendors. This approach reduced the total cost of ownership and the implementation time was significantly shorter.

Ease of Adoption

MIND's solutions were immediately adopted by the market because they are positioned as easy to install, inexpensive to start with and they lower the risk for new carriers in terms of modular function failure or wider disruption to enterprise-wide systems.

Back in the early days of VoIP, it took customers about one-tenth of the time and the cost of a larger billing vendor to deploy the MIND system.

Partner Brand Halo

MIND is a small size company, headquartered in Israel. Their competitors are worldwide leading vendor-brands in the telecom industry. MIND's way of gaining worldwide reputation and market position – at reasonable costs – was to partner with the major network equipment vendors. The value proposition was: integration with MIND products enables the network equipment vendor to complement and enhance their systems and offer their customers a more comprehensive, pre-integrated, low-risk solution. By allocating sufficient resources and, more importantly, significant management attention, MIND built and maintains long-lasting relationships with partner vendors based on this value proposition.

This has proved to be the winning strategy for MIND. The complexity and the ever-changing nature of the billing and service-enabling markets prevented network vendors from developing their own competing products. MIND identified this trend and allocated substantial resources towards its partners, making them and especially their lab managers and sales personnel comfortable with MIND solutions.

Their partnership approach is best exemplified in their relationship with Cisco. MIND is a Cisco partner in both the AVVID and the Ecosystem programs, but it is much more than that. They have an engineer located within Cisco headquarters, providing dedicated support to the lab managers, sales team and account managers of Cisco. This allows MIND a first glimpse of the new and cutting edge development on which Cisco is working. In addition, MIND and Cisco partner for numerous trade shows, where MIND achieves significant and very cost-effective Cisco brand halo.

MIND also invests time and energy in educating and training Cisco personnel about their products and about their joint customers. This enables the Cisco field team to reference MIND's products even in markets where MIND does not have any presence.

Since their partners are big corporations, MIND has tended to establish the partner relationship by starting at the field level and gradually working their way up towards the management level, and not by using the "top-to-bottom" approach.

NEXT STEPS

The objective going forward is to be a leader in the market for billing solutions for multiple IP-based services as the market for these products grows. The strategy includes:

- *Leveraging their brand name recognition and technical expertise.* MIND were one of the first to provide billing and customer care software for IP telephony, introducing MIND-iPhonEX in 1997. That early position in the market and reputation for offering high quality, reliable billing and customer care software has provided them with significant brand-name recognition among VoIP providers. The intention is to leverage the reputation, brand name recognition and expertise to be a leader in the market for billing and customer care software for multiple IP-based services.
- *Enhance alliances with industry leaders.* Co-operative relationships with leading manufacturers of IP telecommunications equipment such as Cisco, Ericsson and Alcatel have already been established. MIND team with these industry leaders in marketing activities, as well as in the research and development and implementation stages of product development and enhancement. These alliances allow them to broaden their marketing capabilities significantly, support new features offered by equipment vendors as these features are introduced to the market and maintain technology leadership over

competitors. The intention is to continue to leverage these alliances in order to solidify and expand market presence.

- *Maintain and expand technological expertise.* MIND's reputation in the market is due in large part to their technological expertise. They make significant investments in research and development to enhance products continually to meet the changing needs in the IP industry. The intention is to continue commitment to technology, both to enhance existing products and to develop new products for growing markets.

- *Offer convergent IP billing products.* As providers of IP-based services continue to broaden their service offerings, MIND believes that they will increasingly need billing products to monitor and bill their customers based on the type and content of the services provided. The intention is to leverage their position and technological expertise in the market for billing and customer care software for IP to be a leading provider of convergent billing products.

- *Expand professional services opportunities.* As IP-based service offerings become more complex, customers increasingly require consulting services, especially for customisation, as well as for project management, installation and training, technical support and maintenance.

MIND can be visited at http://www.mindcti.com

Lateral Thinking to Guide Brand Personality Creative

CORMAC HANLEY
Founder, Oasis Design Group

INTRODUCTION

Although an island nation, the Irish population's fish consumption is relatively low. Making the consumption of "raw" fish appealing was, to say the least, challenging.

In the late 1990s, AYA Restaurant proprietor Yoichi Hoashi decided to introduce this new proposition to Ireland. With the economic boom of the Celtic Tiger period, Irish consumers had changed dramatically – now more affluent, confident and well traveled, with an appetite for new high-quality experiences. The key was to define and create a brand and related customer experience that capitalised on the positive market developments and addressed the negative perceptions with an appealing and engaging customer proposition.

Brand Vision, Mission and Values

The core customer proposition and vision for the AYA brand was to create a widely appealing, contemporary, casual and fun Japanese social dining experience, as an alternative to the traditional pub/bar/restaurant/café. Key brand mission elements were to:

- Introduce an unfamiliar Irish audience to sushi and educate that contemporary Japanese cuisine is "more than" raw fish.
- Establish a flagship "food bar" providing the customer experience in a less demanding atmosphere where customers are not intimidated by the new cuisine and conversation is not disrupted by the arrival of pre-ordered courses.
- Achieve broader market access through franchise of the food bar and Deli sandwich bar style outlets.
- Reinforce product acceptance through making it available in the quality supermarket channel.

Key customer brand values were:

- Appealing
- Fun

- Contemporary
- Quality
- Confidence without elitism.

THE CREATIVE PROCESS

The creative process for translating Yoichi's brand vision, mission and value set into the right brand personality included a novel exercise that involved the project team addressing the following questions:

If AYA were ...

- a drink ... what would it be?
- a band/singer ... who would it be?
- a car ... what would it be?
- a consumer good ... what would it be?

The idea behind this lateral approach was to stimulate a collective creative, provide a reference/guidance to creative execution and to generate ownership of resultant ideas. The results were:

- A drink ... Branson's **Virgin Brand Vodka**
- A band/singer ... **Bjork**
- A car ... **New VW Beetle**
- A consumer good ... **original Sony Walkman.**

The exercise delivered the required creative reference/guidance in terms of a brand personality that visually and verbally communicates *contemporary* with *mass appeal, confidence* and accent on *quality*. In addition there was evidence of a maverick streak, an edge to the brand setting it apart from the rest of the herd. This information was then used to guide the design of the new AYA brand personality.

NEW BRAND PERSONALITY

The new brand personality was evolved creatively over five stages by the Oasis Design Group. Figure 5.11, captures the evolution, which started with the symbol for Japan and gradually transformed into a figure-like character.

Figure 5.11: *Identity Design Process*   Figure 5.12: *New Brand Personality Applications*

1. The Kanji symbol for 'Japan' formed the basis for the logo design.

2. Removing the centre column changed the meaning to 'Big'. Also making the character a unisex shape!!

3. A welcoming smile and a Baseball Cap that doubles as a Wok. In-build the brand values.

4. 1999 Launch Version. The Red circle reinforces the Japan connection.

5. 2004 Evolution; Red square replaces Circle. Revised type. More visual emphasis is now on Symbol.

The revised 2004 interior of AYA provides informal booth type seating adjoining the conveyor

Oasis Design can be visited at http://www.oasisdesign.ie

E-Business Strategy and the Internet

ANGELA KENNEDY
Business Director, Megazyme International Ireland Ltd

INTRODUCTION

Megazyme International, now based in Co. Wicklow, Ireland, develops diagnostic test kits and reagents for the cereals, food, beverages and fermentation industries. The company website was developed and went live in 1994. The company now sells direct to customers or via a network of seven agents worldwide.

In January 2001, the directors of the company planned a redesign of the current website to improve revenue generation. With support from Webtrade, plans were made for the redevelopment of the site and the introduction of e-commerce facilities allowing online payment. The new site was completed and fully operational by May 2001.

Since the redevelopment of the original site, Megazyme revenues have increased substantially. Income from e-commerce now represents nearly 40 per cent of overall sales. The internet proved to be a far more effective means of marketing than traditional channels. Megazyme operates globally without a sales team, highlighting the significance of e-business as an integral part of the overall business strategy.

Redeveloping a website is not without its difficulties and numerous problems need to be overcome. Megazyme, being a small biotechnology company with a current staff of fourteen people, does not have the financial resources to hire its own IT team in-house. Therefore, most of the scientific and administration staff had to learn how to operate the software for downloading and administering online orders, managing the content management system of the site and other processes.

This case study describes Megazyme International's successful experience of e-commerce in a step-by-step approach, illustrating the importance of investing and planning a web operation properly, highlighting the numerous awards the company has won and, most importantly of all, the ROI for the company.

THE COMPANY

Megazyme International is a knowledge-based biotechnology company. It was founded in Australia, in 1989, by Dr Barry McCleary and Angela Kennedy and is now based in Co. Wicklow, Ireland. The company is a globally recognised leader in the development of testing methods for carbohydrates and enzymes, and provides diagnostic test kits and reagents for the cereals, food, beverage and fermentation industries. The company's products are widely used in government research and analytical laboratories, in Universities and by industry customers worldwide such as Guinness, Coors, Anheuser Busch, Unilever, Kellogg's, Weetabix, Quest and H.J. Heinz.

Megazyme is the sole world supplier of more than 80 per cent of the products listed in its current catalogue (250 products in total). These products are developed and produced in its Irish plant in Bray, Co. Wicklow, and are shipped either direct to the customer or through a network of international agents. Where the company has decided to develop and supply products that are already available in the marketplace, the philosophy has been to supply "a superior product at a lower price". Megazyme has representation via a network of seven international agents in Australia, Finland, Holland, Japan, Korea, Spain and Taiwan, and chooses to sell direct to customers in all other countries. The international presence of Megazyme is partly due to the fact that the company prides itself on being "born global". Megazyme test kits have attracted worldwide acclaim for their genuinely innovative nature and the exceptional purity of the enzymes employed. The company exports 98 per cent of its products to over 53 countries across 7 continents, including North America, Europe, Australasia, the Middle East and the Far East. As is the case with many internationally traded services, the core pricing currency is in US dollars in all markets, except for Ireland and the Eurozone, where pricing is in euro.

THE E-COMMERCE LADDER

Step 1 – Use of ICT but not Web

In 1993, Megazyme started with three stand-alone PCs and computerised its internal processes, such as sales, customer service and accounts. This was quickly followed by implementation of the accounting package MYOB (Mind Your Own Business) to control all accounting functionality within the company. The company recognised the competitive advantage that computers offered but did not have access to either e-mail, the internet or a company website.

Step 2 – Limited Success from Web

In 1994, Megazyme established e-mail access and launched its website (www.megazyme.com). When developing its website, the initiative was based on the following principles:

- Megazyme's products matched the needs of an online marketplace
- Internet trading would allow the company to expand its global markets and to lead rather than follow
- The products and services offered by Megazyme matched the net audience
- Some companies in the Megazyme supply chain already used the net
- Potential customers from the scientific and research community were internet savvy and already among the early adopters of the internet as a resource facility.

The internet provided a solution to the time zone problem. More than 90 per cent of Megazyme's customers at that time were based in Europe, North America and Asia, and the time differences made communication by phone very difficult. With e-mail, the communication problem was immediately resolved.

Step 3 – Effective Website

In 1995, a year after launching its website, the company added an ordering facility – eCatalogue – thereby cutting the hefty annual costs of producing and distributing paper catalogues for the European and US markets. By this stage, the internet was being used as an effective marketing and communications tool.

In 1996, the company relocated to Ireland over a single weekend. Thanks to the internet, it was able to cease trading in Australia on a Friday evening and start trading from Bray, Co. Wicklow, the following Monday morning. Although it had taken three months to dismantle the lab and ship products and equipment to Ireland, the actual move from a business and customer point of view happened over a single weekend. Fax and phone numbers were redirected and when customers logged on to the Australian web address, they were automatically shunted straight through to the Irish website. The result was that not even one day's business was lost in the move.

By 1996, the site offered information on new products, international agents, products, purchase details, company profile, standard methods, scientific publications, media news, customer feedback and details of the industries served. One of the prime objectives of the site was to give customers more and better information about the company's products. In 1998, all company technical booklets were converted to condensed files (PDFs) and included in the site at the appropriate positions. This allowed customers to download technical data booklets on each product from the site, using Adobe Acrobat Reader, which ensures that the layout of the booklet is maintained independent of the computer system used to download it (which, of course, is essential).

During 1999, Megazyme incorporated a seamless tracking facility into its website to allow customers to track any shipment online by simply clicking on the Tracking button on the homepage – www.megazyme.com – and typing in the AWB (Airway Bill Number). This identifies the immediate status of the shipment.

Step 4 – Online Catalogue/Payment Systems/CMS

In January 2001, the company undertook a major redevelopment of its site to incorporate additional functionality in eight areas of the site, including design, navigation, content strategy, database, marketing and customer services, online purchasing/administration benefits, online payments system, automatic weight/freight calculation.

The initial design of the site was quite attractive but work was needed to improve and modernise it, improve navigation and search facilities, add FAQs and MSDS information on technical products, change it to a database-driven site, incorporate an online purchasing and online payment facility using Bank of Ireland ClikPay system and incorporate an automatic weight/freight calculation. The Content Management System (CMS) allowed the company to have control over six "live edit" areas of the site, which are continually being updated in-house.

HIGHLIGHTS

Table 5.1 summarises the situation before and after the implementation of the various e-commerce strategies and illustrates the positive substantial impact the redevelopment of the site (May 2001 by Webtrade) has had on the company's "bottom line". The figures are compiled from actual data held by the company.

Megazyme invested €35,000 in new software and in web development costs. They have seen an ROI within four months from increased sales. E-business has been of immense value in developing Megazyme's global reputation. E-commerce has allowed the company to capitalise on the strong net presence it has developed over the past six years. The success of Megazyme's e-business strategy is evidenced by the company receiving several awards, namely:

- Eircom/Irish Independent "Business of the Year 2000" for best use of internet technology
- Dublin Chamber of Commerce "Endeavour Award 2000 for Commerce"
- Spider Awards – Best Use of IT in International Markets (shortlisted to 5 out of 100 companies) (2001).

Table 5.1: *Before and After Implementation of E-Commerce Strategies*

ACTIVITY	BEFORE REDESIGN *(April 2001)*	AFTER REDESIGN *(March 2002)*	CHANGE
Hosting	Indigo	Webtrade	Yes
E-catalogue system		Bespoke system	Yes
Merchant services		BOI ClikPay	Yes
Accounts software	Enterprise Exchequer	Enterprise Exchequer	No
Web traffic analysis	Webtrends	Webtrends	No
Web traffic per month (unique users)	1,524	1,975	+30%
Online sales as a % of total sales per month	21%	27% (€55,672 increase in 4 months)	+48%
Orders per day		Increase of 1–5/day	Yes
Average order value	€640	€760	+19%
New customers per month	18	23	+27%
E-mail address database	Nil	156 in 3 months	Yes
Export countries	36	47	+30%
New products	181	210	+16%
Staff	10	12	+2 increase

BENEFITS OF E-BUSINESS FOR MEGAZYME

By 2003, Megazyme had become an e-business success story:

- 36 per cent of all sales are conducted via the website, directly, and an additional 8 per cent of orders are received electronically (e-mail)
- 50 per cent of all new customers are generated via the web (average of 30 per month)
- Average of 188,220 hits per month (2,790 unique users)
- The company's efficiency and profitability has been transformed through the effective use of internet technologies.

E-business strategy has been central to Megazyme's business objectives and has helped the company to reach new markets, offer high-value products and services, improve the company's competitive position and establish its international reputation. Megazyme can be described as an e-business pioneer for its forward thinking and commitment to e-business.

Step 5 – Integration

In November 2003, Megazyme conducted an IT/e-business audit report and action plan with Arekibo on their current website. This audit was driven by the fact that the company wanted to add more functionality to the site including real-time tracking and status of shipments, CRM tools, integration of back-office systems, increase search engine optimisation/visibility, e-marketing and many other features. The recommendations from the audit were as follows:

1. A full redesign of the existing website to include additional functionality and/or
2. Rebuild a totally new website that is compliant with existing web standards using a combination of XHTML and CSS language, integration of CRM (Application Server) product into new site, updating of online purchasing facilitator, integration of back-office, accounting and FedEx product.

The company has chosen Option 2 since its website does not fully comply with current web standards as outlined by World Wide Web Consortium (W3C).

SUMMARY

The ultimate goal for a company with e-business presence is to achieve maximum customer satisfaction by electronically integrating business processes to improve efficiency and effectiveness. This involves continual updates, which will trigger a series of ongoing practices. Megazyme International is not standing still; it is continually reviewing its site and benchmarking against "best of breed". Empowered with the next phase of this new e-capability, Megazyme will continue to enhance its reputation in setting new standards both scientifically and in the new e-economy.

Megazyme International can be found at http://www.megazyme.com

New Product Adoption

GERRY McCAUGHEY
Managing Director, Century Homes
Ernst & Young Industry Entrepreneur Of The Year ® 2003, Ireland

INTRODUCTION

Founded in January 1990, Century Homes is now the largest housing timber frame (roof trusses, walls, door units, floors) manufacturing business in Ireland and the UK, employing over 320 staff. Century started life in the head of Gerry McCaughey, who as a college undergraduate completed three different projects on "timber frame" – all pointing to factual and technical reasons why all houses should be built this way:

- it halves the builders' time on site
- it saves cost for onsite storage and security
- it reduces likelihood of injury
- it reduces the role of the powerful "block layers"
- it has higher levels of insulation and environmental benefits.

THE MARKET WAS "MORTAR"

However, the house building market was almost all mortar based and none of the timber frame companies in existence at that stage offered the complete house build frames or was able to educate the market.

GETTING TIMBER FRAME ADOPTED

Gerry has done just that. His strategy recognised that the task on hand was akin to that of the four-strand, new-technology adoption task. He had to:

1. *Ensure that the product was of the highest quality*, if it was to be used as a replacement. He therefore has all four quality marks (Q mark, ISO 9001, ISO 14,001, Excellence in People) and he devised innovative and patented processes to underpin and produce that top quality.

2. *Educate the market as to the benefits of timber frame*. He has therefore invested huge personal time and resources in ensuring, for example, that Ireland's new building regulations did not

discriminate against timber frame. He has also spoken extensively about and for timber frame in all media.

3. *Push aggressively out into the market,* working twelve hours a day, seven days a week to sell timber frame to builders (in the early days this was Monday to Friday) and to one-off builds (this was Saturday and Sunday). He sold effectively, targeting initial builders who had previous experience or overseas experience of timber frame. He also understood the key reason why his new technology is often not adopted – it can demand huge process, people and cultural change for the prospective buyer. This needs to be addressed in the sales process.

4. *Now he is deploying the market pull strategy* to carry the business into large scale revenue by branding the business. An early indication of market pull is the 500,000 in sales over the internet in six months.

SUMMARY

Gerry has executed all of these strategy elements and opened a new market in a very traditional and tough sector. Century Homes now has an increasing market share and rising sales revenues. He puts it down to "persistence beats resistance", his fifth strand to ensuring successful new technology.

Century Homes can be visited at http://www.century.ie

World–Class New Product Development

MARTIN McVICAR

Managing Director, Combilift Ltd,
Ernst & Young Entrepreneur Of The Year ® 2001, Ireland

INTRODUCTION

Martin McVicar and Robert Moffett (technical director) formed Combilift Ltd in 1998 with the aim of developing a world-class and leading forklift truck for a significant niche sector – long-load handling – within the material-handling market. The result of their new product development (NPD) process was the world's first engine-powered, all-wheel drive, multi-directional industrial forklift. Their unique solution, using one truck as opposed to the then industry practice of using a combination of side-loaders and counterbalance and narrow-aisle trucks to manoeuvre long and bulky loads around narrow yards, soon found enthusiastic users across diverse industries in the material-handling business around the globe.

Starting with a staff of just three in 1998, the company now employs over 95 people in its 60,000 sq. ft. manufacturing and design facility in Clontibret, Co. Monaghan, and exports to 40 countries via a network of 85 dealerships worldwide. Exports account for 93 per cent of production. Over 2,000 Combilift trucks are in operation worldwide in locations as diverse as Barbados, New Zealand and Iceland.

WORLD-CLASS NPD

At the outset of their NPD process, Martin and Robert set about solving their end customers' key problems, the most important of which was and is to maximise space in storage facilities. The multi-directional capability of the truck means that it can operate in aisles as narrow as two metres, as compared to four metres previously using other trucks, thereby enabling customers to reduce storage space by 50 per cent or to double the amount of stock stored within existing warehouses. In addition to customer storage concerns, the Combilift was also developed to address customer efficiency issues. In this regard, the new truck was developed to operate outdoors on semi-rough terrain as well as indoors and to run on LPG or diesel power to minimise truck downtime for the customer, for example due to battery charging. Many Combilift customers use the trucks in round-the-clock operations. Rigorous quality control standards at the manufacturing plant ensure a finished product that has an excellent maintenance track record.

NPD and Positioning Insights

The Combilift concept was deliberately developed for a niche market (Long Load Material Handling Sector). Niche markets escape the focus and competitive attentions of the "big players". Market needs were carefully identified and the most important selling benefits in each market were then identified, for example:

- In Europe, the space saving by travelling sideways is the key benefit
- In the US, the safer product handling is more important; this can be achieved by travelling sideways with a long load
- In colder climates, for example Scandinavia and Canada, the big advantage of the Combilift is its ability to travel outdoors even in winter snow conditions.

Design parameters for Combilift were discussed in the marketplace with both potential customers and dealers before a detailed design was prepared. To ensure that the design features were correct, they followed the delivery of the first three units that were exported to Norway to get direct customer feedback, both positive and negative.

The Combilift was developed to meet all design safety requirements for Europe and North America at the initial stage.

Distributors were appointed in Norway, Belgium and France during 1998 to initiate commercialisation of the new truck while they continued to focus their efforts on final product development tweaking and testing.

They did not exhibit at international trade fairs during the first two years, to avoid alerting other forklift manufacturers to the Combilift concept and incurring major marketing costs in those early years.

They currently exhibit the Combilift at a number of "application" exhibitions, which attract significant numbers of potential end-users. For example, for timber industry they exhibit at the world international timber trade fair, "Ligna". They avoid, for example, the forklift Material Handling Expo, where there are more potential competitors than potential end-users.

They realised that the French customer generally wants to purchase French products. They therefore branded the Combilift in France as "Combi-Amlat".

For new market entry, their strategy is to find a customer for the product first and then "the good distributor will find you".

Because the Combilift is unique in its operation, they produced for distributors and end users a CD/video of the Combilift in operation. This explained the unique product far better than the best quality brochure.

A distributor must purchase a demo Combilift before they are appointed, to demonstrate their commitment to the product line. Each distributor has a one-year contract with an agreed sales target. If this is not met, it is at Combilift's discretion to extend the contract or not.

The product is always positioned on the benefit for the customer. To that end, three engineers are deployed to prepare warehouse designs for a potential customer (free of charge), showing how much more product can be stored in their building.

Figure 5.13: *The Combilift*

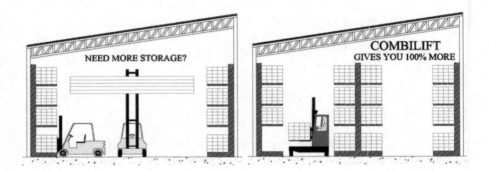

The individual sales person within a distributor's organisation is the key. They have to be motivated to sell a new concept product. Early success in selling a new concept product is critical for a distributor's continued involvement.

Combilift try to sell in the currency of their buyer's country. They sell in euro, sterling, US$, Can$ and Aus$. An end-user always wants to purchase in their currency. A distributor may purchase in your currency but may add on a buffer of 10 per cent for example, to allow for future currency fluctuation. This can mean that your product may be uncompetitively priced by 10 per cent. Expand your product range quickly to achieve maximum distributor commitment.

Combilifts now range in capacity from 2,500kg (5,500Ibs) to 10,000kg (22,000Ibs).

Combilift can be visit at http://www.combilift.com

Marketing through a Manufacturer's Representative Distribution in North America

TERENCE MONAGHAN
Chief Executive Officer, BetaTHERM Sensors

INTRODUCTION

BetaTHERM Sensors was originally established in 1983 in Boston, USA. In 1998, the Irish Management team, led by Terence Monaghan, bought the business from its American founder. With its head office in Galway, Ireland, the company designs and manufactures Negative Temperature Co-efficient Thermally Sensitive Resistors, NTC Thermistors and other electronic components which display a negative change in resistance to an increase in temperature. The products are positioned as superior to other types of heat sensors *vis* their accuracy (+ or -0.05C), responsiveness (200 milliseconds), size (0.35mmOD), long-term stability and operating temperature range (-50C to +250C). The company has a 4 per cent market share of the global NTC Thermistor market. It employs 350 people in Ireland, USA, Poland, Barbados and China and generates roughly half its business from the USA and half from Europe from the following customer segments:

1. **Bio-Medical:** Ablation, thermography, ventilation, dialysis, endovascular cooling and patient monitoring
2. **Aerospace:** Satellite surface sensors and environmental control
3. **Instrumentation and Control:** Blood/DNA analysis, chemical analysis, pH monitoring, liquid, air/gas flow sensing, environmental/meteorological
4. **HVACR:** Air conditioning, immersion probes, commercial refrigeration and boilers
5. **Automotive:** Engine management systems, environmental control and seat heaters
6. **Communications:** Battery chargers, mobile phones, routers and DWDM systems
7. **Consumer:** Insect control, swimming pools, spas and office equipment.

WHY MANUFACTURING REPRESENTATIVES?

For the electronic components industry in the US, buyers prefer to deal with a small, limited number of potential suppliers and they trust the "manufacturer representative" network to provide the consultative advice (directly on small value items or indirectly with a manufacturer on complex larger buys) and product they require. In addition, the representative channel gives immediate and wide territory access.

SETTING UP THE REPRESENTATIVE CHANNEL

BetaTHERM has just completed a seven-stage process to find, appoint and operate eight representative firms (typically two partners, two field representatives and an office administrator) which open up 71 per cent of the addressable market in the USA for its NTC Thermistor product. The steps and stages were as follows.

1. Generate the Potential List of Representatives

For BetaTHERM, the ERA (Electronic Representatives Association) and MANA (Manufacturers Agents National Association) memberships were a key source of firms by territory. Existing representatives were also asked for referrals into new territories. Competitor websites yielded lists, as did websites of "complimentary" product manufacturers. Enterprise Ireland also provided lists.

2. Do Homework on the Listed Representative Firms

A visit to their website tells you a lot in an initial screening. Is the website up to date? What product lines do they currently carry? What territory and markets do they cover? What are the firm background and ownership details? This, together with any other information from existing representatives and complementary manufacturers, gives the prospect listing of representative firms.

3. Get their Attention and Interest

This is best done first by a phone call, rather than a mailing of letters, faxes or e-mails. In a phone call, the objective is to get across the message that (a) your company is looking for representation in their territory and (b) after visiting their website/talking to X in Y company, you see that that they have a good mix of product that may be synergistic to what you are offering.

The phone call (or voice message, if you left one) is then followed by a letter covering the following: the markets and specific prospects they cover that you are interested in; your products that can add value to their existing lines and markets; new market opportunities that your product/customer target opens up for the representative; and finally your statement of commitment to the representative network and the support you will provide to help them succeed.

4. Conduct Personal Interviews

Visit their offices and get the look and feel of their people and their business.

5. Background Checks and Due Diligence

Check customer and principal references.

6. Finalists Factory Visit

A mechanism to test the prospective representative firm's real interest in carrying your product and an opportunity to move the relationship on.

7. Decision and Offer

Those that come closest to meeting the "ideal representative profile" and score highest on the "evaluation forms" in the following areas are offered an agency:

- ability to cover the target territory
- synergy of representative business customer base (to BetaTHERM strategy)
- professionalism of the representative firm and staff
- size of firm's sales
- synergistic "line card"
- mind share/likely attention of representative to you
- desire to carry your products
- "meeting of minds", working together to grow both businesses.

LESSONS LEARNED

Once the representative firms have been appointed, what are the key network management requirements to grow its revenues from zero to target? Amongst the key "do's" are:

- Agree clear annual sales targets with representatives in each territory, based on total sales and growth and agree upfront on reporting requirements.

- Support the network with a dedicated sales team of your own, having them available at all times by phone and in the field with the representatives for at least one week per month. Dedicate also a customer service team to support the representatives on sales order processing, sample requests, literature and so on.
- Run an annual Representative of the Year award – it motivates performance.
- Generate and provide the representatives with qualified and unqualified leads and create effective selling tools for their use in enhancing the sales process for speedy commission earnings. Copy the representatives with all company advertising and PR coverage for your company and products.
- Early success in selling your products is critical to securing the representative's mind share and commitment to your product.
- Most representatives grow their business by selling more products to their existing customers; you have to have very close alignment on mutual end customers therefore. The very good ones will also focus on new customer acquisition.
- You need to fund the representatives' marketing efforts, with a commitment of some $2,000 to $5,000 per month over a six- to twelve-month period.
- You may also have to provide a "draw" facility for the representative on eventual commissions to be earned and pay higher commission in the initial start-up phase over one or two years.
- Share success stories and application notes.

Most importantly, you must positively differentiate yourself from the representative network – chiefly by generating/providing qualified leads, providing effective sales tools, paying commissions in an accurate and timely manner and maintaining simple, regular and valued communications.

Business and Operational Criteria for Hiring Representatives

1. Business age of the candidate
2. Reputation
   - Among customers
   - Among other manufacturers the distributors currently represent
   - Among peers
   - Among trade publications
3. Professional background of key executives
4. Business and managerial stability
5. Financial strength
6. Sales revenue performance

- Overall sales
- Complementary product lines

7. Branch locations
8. Number of active customer accounts
9. Present territorial coverage
10. Complementary manufacturer product lines represented
11. Competitive product lines represented
12. Product variables
   - Technical expertise
   - Newness
   - Knowledge of existing product lines
13. Knowledge of local market conditions
14. Employee quality
15. Managerial "chemistry"
16. Overall condition of facilities

Sales and Marketing Criteria

17. Type of market coverage offered
   - Horizontal
   - Vertical
   - Both
18. Proportion of internal to external salespeople
19. Sales force compensation
20. Sales cycle performance requirement
   - Pre-sale
   - Transaction
   - Post-sale
21. Sales competency
   - Number and quality of salespeople
   - Technical competence of salespeople
22. Sales and marketing aggressiveness
   - Local marketing activities
   - Customer and order pursuit
   - Dealing with their competition
23. Internal sales and marketing support resources and capabilities
24. Ordering and payment policies
25. Customer order fulfilment performance
   - Typical time required for complete delivery of a customer's purchase order
   - Accuracy of shipment of order contents
   - Percentage of out-of-stock occurrences
26. Price integrity

27. Ability to develop new markets
28. Distributor advertising and sales promotional programs
29. Training programs
30. Consent to sign a contract
31. Agreement to accept a sales quota
32. Willingness to share data and local market information
33. Willingness to participate in joint sales and marketing programs
34. Inventory management expertise
35. Adequate inventory commitment
36. Future growth prospects

Coup de Grace Factors that Indicate a Motivated Candidate

37. True desire for your product line
38. Willingness to share key customer list
39. Willingness to commit resources to your product line
40. Existence of a strategic business plan
41. Willingness to participate in strategic business planning with your company

BetaTHERM Sensors can be visited at http://www.betatherm.com

A Winning Product Strategy

FIONAN MURRAY
Chief Executive Officer, LeT Systems Ltd

INTRODUCTION

Waterford based utility software specialist LeT Systems has exploited the opportunity created by deregulation of electricity markets across the world with a very disciplined product-based strategy. A provider of network operations software for the utility industry, LeT Systems is the market leader in the UK and is successfully developing new business in the US, Eastern Europe, South Africa and Asia Pacific markets.

LeT has created a "COTS" (Commercial Off The Shelf) software product specifically for utility network operations. Called eRespond, the software product is now being used by electricity companies that collectively serve a customer base in excess of 30 million consumers worldwide. LeT's strategy to develop "product" to meet customer key needs in an industry sector (without requirement for significant adaptation for use) has been at the core of its marketing strategy.

THE "PRODUCT" STRATEGY

From day one, LeT decided that it would develop a product on the basis that utilities, particularly in the UK, were going to have to meet a much more stringent set of common regulatory requirements. The UK regulator was imposing strict requirements to limit the amount of time consumers could be left without power, with consequential heavy financial penalties if metrics were not met. This meant that utility companies had to find a way to improve network reliability and to demonstrate to the regulator that these levels had been achieved.

After the development of its network operation software to meet these needs, LeT Systems went on to become a major supplier to UK electricity distribution companies. It is now the market leader, with its flagship product, eRespond, being used as the core operational software solution by 70 per cent of the market.

The core "functional" benefits to utility companies of eRespond are improved network operational efficiency, reduced costs and improved customer service. It allows utilities to maintain an accurate picture of their network, to identify faults and outages and to automate the process of workforce management for repairs and maintenance.

As a "product" eRespond has been deliberately developed as "best of breed" – combining the needs, experiences and work practices of a wide range of customers. As a widely deployed solution with reference sites on three continents, prospective customers can see it working before their decision to purchase.

Customers have responded well. The "product" buy enables them to avoid taking risks on bespoke application developments. This assures them of short project timescales, a factor vital in achieving return on investment and meeting business needs. And as part of a user community they can influence LeT's product roadmap, learn from other customers' use of the system and get the benefit of new functionality where the cost of development is being shared.

The ease with which systems integrators can deploy the product, often as part of an integrated solution, is another winning feature of the "product" strategy. LeT's adherence to international and industry standards in integration allow partners' staff to deploy the solution quickly and effectively.

eRespond has also been designed for deployment with partners' technologies such as SCADA (supervisory control and data acquisition) and DMS (distribution management system) used in utilities. This allows the vendors of those complementary technologies to partner with LeT and to leverage the benefit of the combined solution sets.

The eRespond product suite can also be used in conjunction with ERP (enterprise resource planning) systems, such as SAP, in order to more fully integrate planning, reporting and management systems.

"PRODUCT" AS THE ENTRY POINT TO GLOBAL MARKETS AND OTHER INDUSTRIES

The investment in "product" development, rather than a solution tailored to only one or two customers, has paid off for LeT. The company has demonstrated that a single product strategy solving the key, common industry (as opposed to singular company) needs and based upon high quality architecture and programming, meeting international integration standards and designed for ease of operability with allied technologies used in the industry can be the winning marketing strategy and decision.

It has created LeT's market entry point to the utilities market, both in terms of geography and in terms of software solution offer. The product approach allows sets of customers to be marketed, from the highly sophisticated utilities of the UK to the utilities in emerging markets – both keen to make the technology "leap" to current best practice. And its ability to work as a stand-alone solution, as part of a SCADA/DMS offering or as part of an ERP offering has created multiple entry points to those customers. It has also created multi-faceted partnering opportunities as a result.

Having built up its reputation in the UK market, the company has gone on to gain a strong foothold in the US and South African markets and is now developing into Eastern Europe and Asia Pacific markets with its product-based solution. With the "foot-in-door" product sale made, the next generation software product is now being developed with embedded artificial intelligence to increase the decision support available to users.

At present, all of the company's customers are electricity companies but LeT Systems plans to widen this range since its software can also be used by any "wire and pipes" business including gas companies, water companies and waste-water companies. Early market sensing in these new verticals suggests that LeT's product-based approach will transfer successfully.

LeT Systems can be visited at http://www.letsys.com

From a Personal-Based Brand to Leadership Brand Position

PADRAIG O'CEIDIGH
Managing Director, Aer Arann
Ernst & Young Entrepreneur Of The Year® 2002, Ireland

INTRODUCTION

Aer Arann was originally set up in 1970 as an air service to meet the social and community needs of three small islands off Galway on the west coast of Ireland. Padraig O'Ceidigh bought the island-hopping airline in 1994, at which point it had a turnover of €317,000 and had to be restructured immediately to ensure its continued viability.

GREAT BRAND – FIRST ATTRIBUTE

Soon after acquiring the island-hopping airline, Padraig had his "compelling idea" – filling the unmet need in Ireland for an "international regional airline" that would better serve local communities for their point-to-point journey needs within Ireland.

The first hallmark of a great brand was secured – the big idea that captures attention and loyalty.

GREAT BRAND – SECOND ATTRIBUTE

However, at this stage the public saw Aer Arann as a very small airline –flying two nine-seater Britten Norman Islander Aircraft to and from three small islands off the west coast of Ireland. If the compelling idea was to be brought to life, Padraig knew he would have to change this market perception very quickly.

His strategy was therefore to become intimate with the communities to be served and integrate Aer Arann as much as possible into the local areas. He personally brought the "core purpose" and value set of the "international regional airline" brand position to local communities all along the western and south-western counties of Ireland. The brand became a cause and a set of stories told and recounted by Padraig everywhere he went to meet people and in every communication medium available for use by him – newspaper interviews, radio interviews and meetings with local chambers of commerce.

The second hallmark of a great brand was secured – the resolute core purpose of the brand and supporting brand values.

GREAT BRAND – THIRD ATTRIBUTE

The third key attribute that great brands display is an organisation that takes the brand position and values and uses them as management levers to guide all business strategy and decision making. The brand position is first and foremost lived by all staff in the organisation, which in turn creates the platform for consistent and continuing "customer experiences" of the brand. Padraig started this process himself, setting the example for all staff – every day he travelled (and still travels) by Aer Arann from his home in Galway to the Airlines HQ in Dublin airport

The third hallmark is at an advanced stage.

THE HAT TRICK!

Has he succeeded? What impact has the brand position had in the market? From two island-hopper aircraft and a single Shorts 360 aircraft in 1997, Aer Arann has acquired a fleet of ATR 42 and 72 aircraft flying more than 400 weekly flights – now the second biggest operator of such aircraft in Europe, carrying more than 600,000 passengers in Ireland and into more UK destinations than Aer Lingus – the national carrier.

According to leading airline analysts Raymond James and Associates in 2002, "Padraig O'Ceidigh, in our opinion is uniquely positioned to develop a relatively large and leading regional airline in Europe".

Aer Arann can be visited at http://www.aerarann.com

Partnering: A Driver for Innovation and Growth

LIRIO ALBINO PARISOTTO
President, Videolar
Ernst & Young Entrepreneur Of The Year® 2002, Brazil

INTRODUCTION

In the 1980s, the home entertainment market in Brazil was in its infancy when Lirio Parisotto was invited by Sony to Japan as a successful re-seller for the company. Instead of using the trip as a social event, he visited Sony's videotape telecining, subtitling and recording laboratory facilities. With the learnings, he set up a similar plant in Brazil. Thus started Videolar's business of tape translation, recording and subtitling. It also established his formula for growth – partnering and innovation.

Videolar today pioneers DVD copying in Latin America; it is the largest player in CD-R production in the region and the only diskette producer in Latin America. In a market (audio, video and unrecorded media) worth some R$1.5 billion Videolar has captured a market share of 33 per cent. Fifteen years later, Videolar now employs 2,600 professionals and generates a further 1,500 indirect jobs.

PARTNERING WITH "CUSTOMERS"

Videolar's partnership with its key customers is based on a continuously evolving relationship, focused on three key dimensions:

1. Creating and offering products and services fully in line with the new needs and expectations of the sector. There are fifteen international leading players in Videolar's market space and Videolar's strategy is to be in line with what these companies are developing. Videolar participates actively in industry exhibitions and congresses to keep abreast of new developments and the company pays royalties for use in a continuous attempt to bring innovation to Brazil.
2. Videolar invests heavily in information technology to underpin efficient commercial relationships with customers, processing more than 100,000 invoices each month with their studio and music company customers.
3. Videolar continually looks for ways to reduce costs for its customers. In the early 1990s, Videolar centralised product distribution for its customers, offering a warehouse storage facility (30,000 square

meters) and was consequently able to reduce the cost borne by its key partner–customers by 40 per cent. Until that point, all of its customers carried the full costs for distribution of their products. In addition to product storage, customers such as Paramount were able to carry all of their operations in Videolar premises. Other customers such as Warner Music, Disney, Warner Video, Fox and Columbia carry out some of their operations in the main offices of Videolar.

PARTNERING WITH "INNOVATORS"

In addition to partnering with customers, Videolar has developed key relationships and important contracts for technology transfer and patent purchase from large multinational companies. With Philips International B.V. (Netherlands) and Sony (Japan), Videolar obtained licences to manufacture sound CDs, CD-ROMs, DVDs and CD-Rs. Videolar entered into an agreement with the consortium DVD 6C (USA and Japan) and obtained from Toshiba Corporation a CSS (Content Scramble System) license for DVD cryptography. From Macrovision (England), Videolar imported technology to curb copying of CD-ROMs, DVDs and VHSs. From California Video Center – Time Warner Entertainment Company (USA) Videolar brought DVD authoring technology. These were key contracts and agreements for Videolar's entry into this market segment.

PARTNERING WITH "COMPETITORS"

In the 1980s, Videolar made associations with thirteen competitors in their market segment, several of which were later merged into the company. This strategy added to growth in significant terms.

PARTNERING WITH "KNOWLEDGE ORGANISATIONS"

Videolar also has partnerships with knowledge organisations that can contribute to its growth through innovation strategy. For example, they have a partnership with FIA-USP, one of the best business administration schools in Brazil, to improve qualification of its managers. In 2003, the institution created and taught a focused tailor-made MBA for 48 company managers. Videolar also sends employees for training in new technologies; for example, to WAMO (Warner Advanced Media Operations) in the USA on DVDs; to Germany and England about CD-Rs and operations; and to Japan about VHS, among others.

Videolar can be visited at http://www.videolar.com

International Marketing and Expansion: A "Local Global" Strategy

MARIO MORETTI POLEGATO
President, Geox S.p.A.
Ernst & Young Entrepreneur Of The Year® 2002, Italy

INTRODUCTION

Geox S.p.A. was established in the mid-1990s as a small company and after just a few years became a major player in the shoe industry. In 2001, growth in excess of 50 per cent in sales of 3.7 million pairs of shoes generated €150 million revenue. In 2002, it sold 4.7 million pairs of shoes and in 2003 sales were expected to reach some 6.5 million. Geox is number one in Italy and is one of the world's ten biggest companies producing casual footwear. Geox generates 35 per cent of its revenues from over 68 countries around the globe, the top markets being Germany, France and Spain.

The company's success is founded on an innovative technology developed by Mario Moretti Polegato – "the shoe that breaths". The rubber outer sole of Geox shoes has pores through which air flows in and out and a membrane placed in the sole absorbs and removes sweat from the shoe, while at the same time stopping water from leaking inside. Its mission statement is "to convert an increasing number of people into consumers of breathing products" and marketing execution is guided by three corporate brand values:

1. Geox "breathes" is a brand duty, a corporate belief and a product mission
2. Research and technological development allow Geox to generate patent-based products (footwear and accessories) for a differentiated market positioning
3. More than 10 per cent of revenues is spent on communicating with the Geox customer, who is transnational.

THE LOCAL–GLOBAL STRATEGY

Geox drives its international expansion with four key marketing strategies:

1. Enter a market initially by way of licencing agreement with retailers, selling a multi-brand and multi-national shoe range at similar price-point to the Geox shoe price in the major cities.
2. Establish the mono-brand Geox shops – carrying their men's, women's

and children's shoes and clothes in the same locations and cities in that country. Shop numbers are nearly doubling every year: in 2000, there were 32; in 2001, there were 68; in 2002, there were 130; and at the end of 2003, there were 200 Geox shops worldwide.

3. Partner with a local shoe manufacturer to adapt the Geox "technology shoe" to the local fashion and taste to produce a Geox "local" shoe that complements the standard Geox technology shoe range.

4. Invest in communication programmes to educate the country market as to the benefits of the Geox technology shoe – health and hygiene benefits – and thereby shift buyer decision making beyond just a "fashion" buying decision.

The Strategic Importance of a Single Brand Name Geox Shop

- It represents a privileged window-displaying option for all the fashion footwear and clothing collections (for men, women and children).
- The decision to establish all Geox shops in the most exclusive streets of the most important capitals around the world places Geox products at a medium/high range.
- The importance of the lay out: single brand name Geox shops have been designed to communicate the foundation of the product: technology and innovation. The choice of the materials used to build the shops (glass and steel) is not at all casual but is the result of logical reasoning laid down by the company's strategy. The idea is to have Geox shops perceived as a real and true research workshop. This is the explanation behind the use of light coloured materials and glass, the highest expression of transparency and modernity.
- Retail innovation: Geox shops are designed to offer a new consumer experience. Unlike normal "civil" shoe-shops, Geox shops are structured in a way that enables the client to touch all the collections, leading them to follow a different buying route that is not tied to the classic client/shop assistant relation.
- A new figure is born – "the consultant": the shop assistant leaves the client maximum liberty of movement and does not interfere with the decision/choice procedure: he will only assist the client if he is specifically consulted by him (if the client needs detailed explanation on the products) or he may even just finalise the purchase.

Geox and Communication

One advertising medium (innovation and technology) modified according to the different target reference (men, women, children).

Example: Child Segment

Since its foundation, Geox philosophy has always been based on the strategic importance of communication and on the necessity of modifing the key message to the different target in the best way. To reach the child segment target, they needed to create an appropriate communication. Thus was born Magic Geox, a fantasy character created to communicate Geox philosophy and, at the same time, to spread a new "functionality" of shoes: not only design and fashion but also wellness. All this is "the shoe that breaths". Magic Geox's adventures were born in comics available in the Geox shops. During every collection, they published a new episode. A website has been created – www.magicgeox.com – that has carried the inventor of "the shoe that breaths" from paper to web. Nowadays, all child fans of Magic Geox can become fond of his adventures also on web looking at the new 3D cartoon.

Figure 5.14: *Images from a Geox Shop*

Figure 5.15: *Magic Geox and his Website (www.magicgeox.it)*

Geox can be visited at http://www.geox.com

Brand Building – Without the Budget

RICHARD REED
Co-Founder, Innocent Drinks
Ernst & Young Young Entrepreneur Of The Year ® 2003, United Kingdom

INTRODUCTION

In the last twelve months, Innocent Drinks has been the fastest growing "smoothie" brand in the UK. Brand awareness has grown by 28 per cent in a year – reaching 41 per cent national awareness and market share has grown from 14 per cent to over 30 per cent in four years. Innocent Drinks are now available in over 4,000 outlets, including all Sainsburys and Waitrose stores, Starbucks, Boots, Eat and many other independent retailers.

In 2002, Innocents Drinks became the top smoothie brand in four of the five major multiples in which they are stocked.[2] Turnover for 2004 is running at an annualised Stg£11m.

AND THEIR SECRET …

This could not have been achieved without effective, creative and inexpensive marketing. Ruthless creativity and using every channel available, however small or unusual, can achieve great results. Consistency of tone and integration is also extremely important. However, marketing can only ever be as focused or powerful as the overall vision for the company and that is why Innocent work hard to ensure that everyone at "Fruit Towers" (the head office!!) is aware of and involved at some level in guarding and growing their brand.

CREATIVE, NOT CONVENTIONAL MARKETING COMMUNICATIONS

Innocent did not have the cash to do marketing in more conventional ways. They had to come up with creative alternatives that still achieved the goal of building their brand. This meant using every medium available to communicate with their consumers: from the ever-changing copy on the labels; to the delivery vans with horns and tails and a special button that makes a mooing noise; to inviting their consumers to call on

---

2. *Source*: AC Nielsen data

the "Banana Phone" whenever they feel a bit bored; and, in 2002/2003, the "Dancing Grass Van" – a sampling vehicle that is an ice-cream van covered in astroturf and daisies that can dance. Every opportunity for low-cost, high-impact marketing that creates an invaluable word of mouth buzz about their products is considered.

Figure 5.16: *The First Ever Dancing Grass Van to Tour the Streets of the UK and Ireland in 2002*

MARKETING STRATEGY AND MIX

Every single element of the Innocent marketing strategy has to pass the "Innocent" test:

- Is it natural?
- Is it honest?
- Is it engaging?
- Is it the best way to communicate our messages to this audience?
- Is it cost-effective?

Figure 5.17: *Nina Talking to a Consumer on the Banana Phone*

Although seemingly simple questions, they are the "Innocent" way of ensuring that their consistent tone across everything from delivery vans to adverts on the tube and that they never do something just because that is how everyone else has always done it. Hereunder are the key marketing mix elements:

Packaging: to communicate with the people they love the most, their consumers.

- Innocent constantly change label copy – last year saw the number of different labels in circulation at any one time increase to 32 every 3 months
- Packaging is used to channel relevant and timely messages at a time when they have their consumers' undivided attention
- Packaging creates the opportunity to invite customers to call the banana phone or pop in to visit Fruit Towers.

Sampling: delivery vans and Innocent angels to give consumers a unique brand and product experience.

- Actually getting drinks in people's hands is critical to ongoing success
- Innocent angels are well trained to ensure they (as well as the vans) communicate clear messages about who Innocent are
- Customers enjoy pressing the buttons that make the cows go moo and the grass van dance – they get involved with the brand
- The Dancing Grass Van toured the UK and Scotland sampling over 1.3 million people in 2002. It was so successful that another one was built and both are still touring the UK, Scotland and Ireland (in summer 2004 they expect to reach a further 2 million consumers).

Consumer care: strive for consumer infatuation, not just satisfaction.

- The Banana Phone consumer hotline encourages people to ring and have a chat if they are bored
- Customers are encouraged to pop in and visit Fruit Towers
- Any customer who has a bad Innocent experience is sent a case of "sorry smoothies" to arrive the next day
- All letters and e-mails to the "hello" inbox are answered within twenty-four hours
- Little things do not cost much at all, but they make an enormous difference and definitely add richness to everyone's Innocent experience.

PR: media and press coverage is paramount.

- Over 271 articles have been written about Innocent, including mentions in *Vogue*, the *FT Magazine* and being voted the best smoothie on BBC2's *Food and Drink*
- For every Stg£1 spent, Innocent created a multiple of 6.7 in return.

Advertising: retailers must feel Innocent are putting the maximum possible into supporting the brand and letting even more consumers know who they are.

- January 2003 saw a medium-weight advertising campaign in Dublin on the DART and bus sides. This acted as a test for a summer 2004 advertising campaign running in ten key urban areas.

Company literature: some nice words and badly drawn pictures go a long way.

- Literature is given to retailers to display and give out in their shops and is also given out directly to consumers
- Company literature tells the story of Innocent in the Innocent tone, the tone that carries through everything that their consumers will see – the website, the labels, the books and even their grown-up recipe book
- Literature is relatively cost-effective to produce but gives out very strong and clear messages about what sort of company Innocent is and how they like to do business.

Website: Innocent designed and built the kind of website that they would like to use.

- The website reflects and magnifies everything that Innocent stands for as a company and as a brand
- The weekly web news has over 2,000 subscribers
- Like the labels, the site is continually updated.

Figure 5.18: *The Innocent Website*

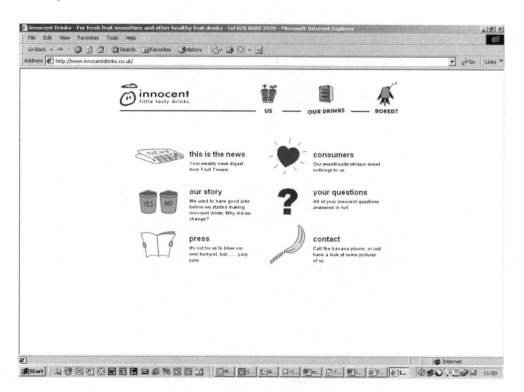

Doing New Things their Way

Innocent looks for totally new channels to reach their "nice consumers". Another of their engaging and innovative ways is their festival in Regent's Park for 40,000 people. It is called Fruitstock and has several objectives:

- To say a big thank-you to all of their 4,000 outlets, everyone has been invited to come along and spend some time in the "Very Nice People" area equipped with lots of nice deckchairs, free drinks and food
- To have a nice fourth birthday party for everyone at Innocent and all of their customers and suppliers
- To have a major free event that Innocent can invite all of their regular consumers to as a way of thanking them for buying their drinks
- To get the Innocent brand out into a major park in London, in the press, on adverts and reach some new consumers.

Figure 5.19: *Fruitstock*

come to fruitstock
an innocent festival

a weekend of lovely music in
Regent's Park - 9th & 10th August

Internal Marketing – Living the Brand

- Set up by three friends with basic principles of being absolutely passionate and hard working – but having fun along the way.

- Their key is motivated and excited employees who become amazing ambassadors for the brand.
- All company Monday-morning meetings each week and all company six-monthly meetings discuss long-term goals to ensure that everyone knows what everyone is up to and how they personally can affect and drive Innocent's future success.
- All get their own bowls and free cereal, fruit, tea and coffee and once a year they all go away skiing together.

SOCIAL PROJECTS

- They believe it is important to run a sustainable business in which everybody believes.
- Innocent distribute drinks to the homeless.
- They fund an NGO called "Women for Sustainable Development" in India. A percentage of smoothie profits go towards buying mango trees and a percentage of the thickie profits go towards buying new cows.
- They sponsor and plant little "Innocent forests" in major cities.

SUMMARY

In summary, Innocent shows how an appealing brand and tone that is communicated creatively and consistently and that is "lived" in all customer interactions – whether that is talking to consumers on the phone, selling in to a new outlet or driving a delivery vehicle – can deliver high market impact at relatively inexpensive marketing cost – less than £100,000 stg.

Innocent Drinks can be visited at http://www.innocentdrinks.co.uk

Keeping the Brand Relevant and Differentiated

LES SCHIRATO
Chief Executive Officer, Cantarella Bros. Pty Ltd AUSTRALIA
Ernst & Young Entrepreneur Of The Year ®
— Retail, Consumer & Industrial Products 2001, Australia

INTRODUCTION

Les Schirato heads the Cantarella Bros. group of companies in Australia – a top 500 privately owned business and major market leader generating $A90 million in revenues. The group's two key coffee brands – Vittoria and Aurora – account for one in every three cups of pure coffee drunk at home in Australia every day.[3] That represents over one million cups a day.

An ancient Greek military formation – the Phalanx Strategy – is used to symbolise the group's mission statement. Its brands are the group's shields and the strategy dictates that, as a group, people are a far greater force than individuals.

"Building brands – in step together with our customers, for greater profits."

Building brands for Les Schirato has meant continuously developing and adjusting the brand positioning to ensure that the brands retain their visibility, relevance and appeal as the marketplace and target audience evolve and change. From 1958, Vittoria pioneered espresso-style coffee in the Australian market and was a key player in the development of cafe society to what it is today. As the market evolved in terms of needs and levels of knowledge and sophistication the business evolved the positioning of the brand and used different marketing media accordingly.

EVOLVING BRAND POSITION AND COMMUNICATION

The positioning and marketing of Vittoria Coffee over its brand life has had several distinct phases which can be outlined as:

Stage One: 1958–1980

Market

Australia was a nation of instant coffee and tea drinkers. Pure coffee

---

3. *Source*: AC Nielsen Scantrack – MAT to 21/12/03 – Tonnes

available in Australia at that time was poor quality – a light roast.

Marketing Triggers

A burgeoning Italian migrant population to Australia post-WWII generated a demand for a true espresso-style pure coffee brand – roasted in Australia. At the time, this was niche market.

Positioning

"Vittoria coffee is your coffee."

Targets

Italian migrants only.

Channels

- Continental delis
- Italian restaurants
- Coffee lounges

Media

- Bus advertising, migrant newspapers, for example *La Fiamma*
- Earliest radio advertising: 4KQ Brisbane 1960–1977
- Editorial in magazines

Results

Coffee sales growth and image of Vittoria increase enabling entry into supermarkets.

Stage Two: 1980s

Market

An idea! Sell Italian-style pure coffee to Australians via the supermarkets – a new retail channel for pure coffee.

Marketing Triggers

Competitors had entered the market for espresso coffee targeted at Italian migrants and subsequently sales growth had slowed. Australians had adopted espresso coffee when served in coffee lounges as the "cappuccino" but continued to use instant coffee at home. The idea was to expand the demand from coffee lounges to a retail market demand, by having pure coffee available in supermarkets – the traditional Australian retail channel.

Positioning

"Vittoria – Making Italian style famous in Australia."

No other coffee company achieved the cut through in advertising and promotion that Vittoria was able to achieve.

Targets

Non-migrant Australians.

Channel

Supermarkets.

Media

- Point of sale/in-store
- Billboards
- Cafe signage

Results

By using a non-traditional supermarket category (i.e. the fruit and vegetable section in supermarkets), Vittoria was the first espresso pure coffee sold in supermarkets. Vittoria forged the beginning of a category, which is now worth over $A80 million annually.[4]

Stage Three: 1980s–Early 1990s

Market

Other imported coffees and locals piggybacked Vittoria's success and started to make gains into supermarkets, espresso lines proliferated and there was the advent of "me too". Vittoria continued to dominate the cafe sector.

Market Triggers

There was increased competitive activity in the retail segment as category

---

4. *Source*: AC Nielsen Scantrack Data

grew. Vittoria's unique position in the cafe market was secured with cafes using heavily branded "Vittoria brand".

Positioning

"Bring home the coffee they serve in cafes."

For the market, pure coffee originated in cafes and many Australians were still enjoying "Vittoria" in cafes, so it was only natural that they would want the same great flavour when enjoying pure coffee at home. Competitors could not make this claim.

Figure 5.20: *Vittoria Cafes*

Targets

Cafe society – enjoy more coffee at home.

Media

- Billboards
- Radio – endorsement Mike Carlton, John Laws

Results

Vittoria increased its market leadership position in the retail segment.

Stage Four: Late 1990s–2003

Market

- Explosion of cafes
- Advent of cafe culture
- Many brands
- Rise of trendy boutique coffees

Market Triggers

Challenge: Vittoria was perceived as being too successful. There was market clutter – many brands in the market. Consumers were confused about which coffee to purchase at a retail level. Vittoria faced loosing its market leadership position.

Positioning

"Where our expertise is still a family tradition."

Vittoria's family ownership, history and expertise in Australia could not be matched by other coffee companies. Consumers could rely on Vittoria as the experts, while other trendy boutique companies came and went. The introduction and promotion of the "Vittoria Coffee College" via media tours generated PR coverage to support the "expertise" value of the brand.

"Award winning cafes and restaurants choose to serve Vittoria Coffee."

Australia's top chefs were the toughest food critics – they only purchased quality for their restaurants and they only served Vittoria and they won awards.

Targets

Consumers who have an unswerving commitment to quality and timeless style – not into short-term trends and fashion. Top chefs and 5-star hotels targeted.

Media

Advertising and advertorials of award winning restaurants in con-junction with the Vittoria brand. Sponsorships of food-related events (i.e. awards) and Italian cultural events – the arts. PR to support the Coffee College. Promotions at individual supermarket accounts. Pure coffee category initiatives at point of sale – education, simplify, cafe feel. Bonus packs (20 per cent more free). Coffee making "kits" to encourage more consumers into the pure coffee market. Radio live reads to tie in with award winning advertising, cafes, hotels.

The "White Coffee Bean" April Fool's Day full-page advertisement in the *Sydney Morning Herald* generated consumer calls, each of whom received a Vittoria gift pack for being good sports. It also generated world-wide radio, TV and newspaper commentary.

Figure 5.21: *The "White Coffee Bean"*

Clients are supported and included in print, radio and TV promotional activity. The "award winning restaurant" campaign engages client restaurants in brand build.

Figure 5.22: *The "Award Winning Restaurant" Campaign*

Results

Vittoria retained market leadership position and increased growth and market lead on main competitor. Vittoria viewed by retail trade as key partner in pure coffee segment.

Vittoria can be visited at: http://www.vittoria.com.au

GLOSSARY OF TERMS

Above the line	Paid-for advertising.
Account management	Process of managing the needs of a client.
Adoption (product)	The categories of consumer who will understand and buy the innovative new product in each of the adoption stages from innovator to early adopter to the laggard.
Advertising	Promotion in a paid-for media, such as press or radio.
Advertorial	An advertisement made to look like a news story.
AIDA	Attention, interest, desire, action as the results in the consumer's mind on foot of advertising or promotion.
Audience	All people, households, organisations that read, hear or view a marketing communication.
Below the line	Advertising or promotion not carried out through an advertising agency for commission payment and includes direct mail and point of sale displays.
Brand	Set of physical attributes of a product or service, together with the beliefs and expectations surrounding the brand that are evoked in the mind of the audience.
Brand communications	The integrated communication set that creates brand "awareness" (advertising), brand "interest" (collateral), brand "desire" and buying "action" (personal selling).
Brand management	The use of the "marketing mix" for the brand.
Brand mission	How the business will achieve its brand vision.
Brand name	The verbal identifier of a brand.
Brand personality	The brand's visual (symbol, typeface, logo, colours) and verbal (name, tag line, stories) elements that are used in all brand communications.
Brand platform	The collective statements of the brand vision, mission and values that are used to create the brand personality.
Brand values	What the consumer really "values" in how

	their need is met and these values are then used to guide all decision making by the brand owner.
Brand vision	What the brand stands for in the market, crucially *vis* a key customer need that is unmet or not currently met satisfactorily.
Business strategy	The means towards achieving stated business aims.
Business to business (B2B)	Buyer and seller are not a personal consumer.
Business to consumer (B2C)	Buyer is a personal consumer.
Buying behaviour/ process	The process that would be buyer goes through in deciding whether to buy or not.
Buying risk	The personal, reputational, financial risk to the buyer in making the wrong buying decision.
Category	How the consumer groups and classifies products.
Channels	Methods used to communicate and interact with an audience.
Collateral	Printed or presentational material of an informational or sales nature, used in the sales process.
Competitive advantage	Product, proposition or benefit that puts a company ahead of its competitors.
Consideration (set)	The limited number of product/providers that a consumer will consider getting involved with in the buying process.
Consumer	An individual who buys and uses a product or service.
Copywriting	Creative generation of written content.
Corporate identity	The "character" of the company as perceived in the minds of the audience.
Corporate reputation	The mix of ethos, identity, image that go to make up market respect for the company and confidence in its conduct.
Creative	Generating a visual and/or verbal representation that is appealing to the buyer's buying behaviour.
CRM	Cohesive and holistic management of contacts and interactions with customer segments.

Customer satisfaction	Fulfilling expectations in terms of quality and service, in relation to the price paid.
Cross selling	Encouraging existing customers to buy other products or services.
Customer attitude	Beliefs and feelings.
Decision Making Unit (DMU)	The group of people in an organisation that make the final buying decision.
Differentiation	Unique element to brand or product/service that makes it stand out in the marketplace from competitors.
Direct mail	Delivery of a marketing proposition via the postal service.
Direct marketing	All mediums that carry a marketing communication to a target audience – post, telephone, e-mail.
Distribution	Moving the product from the manufacturer to the supplier/retailer and consumer.
Diversification	Increase in the range of products, customers or geographies served.
E-marketing	Use of the internet or intranet for marketing communications.
Emotional Selling Proposition (ESP)	Unique emotional associations formed by consumers with particular products or services.
Entrepreneur	Someone who sees opportunity first and then goes about gathering the resources to make it happen.
External analysis	Study of a company's external marketing environment, such as customers, competitors, social and economic trends.
FMCG	Fast-moving consumer goods.
Focus groups	A small group of consumers guided through discussion on a topic under research.
Four Ms	Money, materials, machine and manpower that are available to a business.
Four Ps	Product, price, place and promotion that are the "marketing mix" used to market a brand or product/service.
Fulfilment	Information, material or response to a reader, listener or viewer request for more information.

Innovation	New product, services or processes that increase value.
Internal analysis	Study of the business's internal resources to gauge its strengths and weaknesses.
Involvement	The steps a consumer must take and the interactions they must have to buy a product or service with confidence.
Impression	An impression online is made when an ad is displayed once, in print material, an impression is made when one audience member sees it.
Integrated marketing communication	Use of a full mix of all appropriate (above and below the line) marketing communication disciplines, media and vehicles in a co-ordinated campaign that is designed to achieve a set of objectives.
Key Account Management (KAM)	Process to manage the needs of key customers.
Logo	The visual identifier of a brand, usually a graphic or symbol or group of letters.
Logotype	Brand name or company name rendered in a specified graphical style/typeface/colour.
Market development	Offering existing products to new customers/types.
Market entry	A new product for a new or existing market.
Market penetration	More product into existing market.
Market research	Gathering and analysing information about customers, competitors and marketing environment for strategy formulation and decision making.
Market segmentation	Subgroups of consumers that share common buying attitudes or requirements and that respond to distinct market mix programmes.
Marketing	The strategic management process for identifying, anticipating and satisfying customer requirements on a sustainable and profitable basis.
Marketing audit and analysis	Study of the business's internal resources, strengths and weaknesses and its external

	customer, competitor and marketing environment.
Marketing communications	All methods of visual and verbal interaction with an audience.
Marketing mix	The combination of marketing actions that influence a consumer's buying behaviour towards the company and/or brand. These "actions" are the four ps of product, price, place and promotion; plus people, process and physical evidence.
Marketing myopia	Excessive "product" focus that leads to lack of understanding of the "customer".
Marketing planning	The strategic management process of marketing audit and analysis, marketing strategy formulation and marketing-mix programmes.
Marketing plan	The result of marketing planning whereby the current market situation and the relationship between marketing objectives (where we want to go), marketing strategies (how we get there) and marketing actions (who does what, when and at what cost/resource use) are fully documented and agreed by the business.
Marketing strategy	The methods by which marketing objectives will be achieved.
Mass marketing	Using mass media for marketing communication.
Mission statement	Summary of a businesses philosophy and direction.
Media plan	Clear articulation of the media types and schedule for communication with an audience.
Media release	Company or brand information distributed to all media, beyond just "press".
New Product Development (NPD)	The process for translating consumer needs and wants into new products and services that fit the business's brand and resource capability.
Niche marketing	Marketing to a segment of consumers.
Opt-in e-mail	E-mail to lists of people who have been asked and have agreed to receive

	e-mailings about the topic, product or service.
Personal selling	One-to-one interaction between a seller and a buyer.
Physical evidence or proof	That which the consumer can actually see or experience.
Place	The ways the consumer or retailer get the product or service.
Positioning	Creating a preference in the consumer's mind for your product/service or brand and above that of a competitor.
Product	What the consumer perceives as the distinctive benefits being offered to meet their key needs, in a different or better way to other providers.
Promotion	Advertising, personal selling, public relations, direct marketing, packaging and sales promotions.
Public relations	Explaining the businesses brand or product, establishing and protecting its reputation, influencing stakeholder audiences.
Pull promotion	Getting the consumer to "demand" the brand or product, i.e. they come to us.
Push promotion	Going to the consumer with the brand or product, i.e. we go to them.
Qualitative research	Subjective in nature and enquiry; does not rely on statistical analysis.
Quantitative research	Collected objective data that can be subjected to statistical analysis.
Reach	The audience number or percentage that sees a marketing communication.
Recognition	The ability of an audience member to recall an ad or a campaign.
Relationship marketing	Using a relationship, rather than a product/ transactional approach to generating a lifetime value from the consumer.
Sales promotion	Techniques to engage a consumer and hasten a buying transaction, for example discount coupons, free gifts, etc.
Sponsorship	Specialised form of sales promotion and build of relationship with specific audience.
SWOT analysis	Internal assessment *vis* strengths and

	weaknesses of the business and external assessment of market opportunities and threats.
Tag line	Captures the brand position in a sentence of ten words or less.
Targeting	Selecting and then addressing a particular audience with a distinct marketing-mix programme.
Telemarketing	Use of telephone/call centre in outbound or inbound marketing campaigns.
Testimonial	Endorsement by a customer or retailer/wholesaler of the brand or product service position.
Trade marketing	Marketing to retailers and wholesalers.
Unique Selling Proposition (USP)	The benefit highly prized by the buyer that is not offered or matched fully by a competitor.
Value proposition	The set of benefits prized by the buyer in meeting their needs and desires.

References

Enterprise Ireland, *Doing Business in Japan – A Guide for Irish Technology Companies.*

Enterprise Ireland, *EUR-Open for Business: A Presence in Europe.*

Enterprise Ireland, *Start Up and Marketing in the USA – A Guide for Irish Technology Companies.*

Hart, Norman, Norman Hart Associates, *The Marketing Communications Audit: A Company Self-Assessment*, Cambridge Strategy Publications.

Hofstede, Geert (1991) *Cultures and Organisations: Software of the Mind – Intercultural Cooperation and Its Importance for Survival*, McGraw Hill, New York.

Kotler, Philip (2001) *Kotler on Marketing: How to Create, Win and Dominate Markets*, Simon & Schuster UK Ltd.

Marcus, Aaron, Aaron Marcus and Associates Inc. and Emilie West Gould (2000) *Cultural Dimensions and Global Web User-Interface Design: What? So What? Now What?* Adjunct Lally School of Management, Rensselaer Polytechnic Institute.

Porter, Michael E. (1980) *Competitive Strategy: Techniques for Analyzing Industries and Competitors*, Free Press.

Roberts, Edward B. (1991) *Entrepreneurs in High Technology*, Oxford University Press.

Ryans, Adrian, More, Roger, Barclay, Donald and Terry Deutscher (2000) *Winning Market Leadership, Strategic Market Planning for Technology-Driven Businesses*, John Wiley & Sons Canada Ltd, Figure 4.4.

Varey, Richard J. (2002) *Marketing Communication Principles and Practice*, Routledge.

Wood, James B. with Larry Rothstein (1999) *The Next Level*, Perseus Books.

Index